To Harness the Wind

Steam-Powered Side-Wheel Tugs Towing a Clipper Ship.
Photograph of a painting by Edward Heidvogel

$\mathcal{H}$To arness the $\mathcal{W}$ind

A Short History of the Development of Sails

Leo Block

Naval Institute Press
Annapolis, Maryland

Naval Institute Press
291 Wood Road
Annapolis, MD 21402

Library of Congress Cataloging-in-Publication Data
Block, Leo, 1920–
To harness the wind : a short history of the development of sails /
Leo Block.
        p. cm.
    Includes bibliographical references and index.
    ISBN 1-55750-209-9
    1. Sails—History. I. Title.
VM532.B56 2002
623.8'62—dc21

                                        2002007012

Printed in the United States of America on acid-free paper ⊗
10 09 08 07 06 05 04 03   9 8 7 6 5 4 3 2
First printing

Illustration credits: Cau Uyen, figures 1–43 and 92; Ken A.
Goldenberg, figures 44–91

*To my wife, Shirley, and
to the Dana Point racing sailors who have
provided me with many enjoyable hours on the water.*

Contents

Introduction

Human beings were sailors generations before they invented the wheel or straddled a horse, according to Richard Mansir in his *Modelers Guide to Ancient and Medieval Ships to 1650*. Indeed, humans became sailors when they first stood upon a floating log or raft and noticed that they were traveling faster in a downwind direction. Next, they probably used a large leaf from a palm tree, and later, animal skins between a frame of twigs to create the first true sail. Gradually, through the centuries, humans progressed from sailing only downwind, to sailing across the wind, and finally against the wind.

Initially, a person could sail only downwind, the direction in which the wind is blowing. Paddles and, later, oars were utilized to propel a vessel across the wind and against the wind. To row the vessel against a strong wind was a laborious task and could even be impossible against an exceptionally strong wind. Therefore, the objective of improving the performance of a sailing vessel was not only to make it sail faster, but also to make it sail across the wind and as close as possible toward the direction from which the wind was blowing (as best as possible sailing against the wind, or to windward).

Improvements in performance under sail were not limited in the size, shape, and orientation of the sail. The length-to-beam ratio of the hull, the smoothness of the vessel's bottom, the expanse of freeboard (the distance from the waterline to the deck), the method of steering, and other factors had a significant effect on the performance of a vessel under sail.

Sail development probably occurred simultaneously in several geographic areas; however, we have documentation of this development only in the areas of ancient Egypt, the Mediterranean, and Western Europe. The Egyptians provided us with vases and wall paintings depicting sailing vessels and even a complete vessel in one of the Egyptian tombs. We also have good data on

Viking vessels. Not all Vikings were buried at sea; some were buried in shallow trenches—along with their armor and resting in their longships. Then the trenches were covered to form mounds. Additionally, tapestries of medieval Europe provided a description of the sails used in a particular era; and images of sailing ships were stamped on coins as well. Thus, we have a fairly good description of the types of sails used as Western civilization developed.

From other parts of the world, our history and description of sailing craft starts from the arrival there of the early explorers. The earliest description we have of the Chinese junk was provided by Marco Polo in A.D. 1298. At that time, the junk was already a sophisticated sailing vessel, but we do not know the exact story of its origin; and as for other types of vessels, the Polynesians of the Pacific had sailing vessels that would sail to windward before the arrival of the white man.

Although humankind's mastery of the technology of sailing gradually progressed through the centuries, prior to the thirteenth century the limited sailing capability and rudimentary knowledge of navigation, allowed mostly coastal voyaging and sailing to adjacent islands and peninsulas. The breakthrough in the art and science of sailing occurred late in the thirteenth century when the advances in sail design made by the Europeans were combined with the nautical achievements of the Mediterraneans. This fortuitous union was the inception of what came to be known as the Great Age of Sail.

The combined European-Mediterranean sail proficiency produced a sail arrangement that allowed ships to make prolonged ocean voyages, leading to the Age of Discovery in which new lands and sea routes were discovered. This era was followed by the Great Age of Sail, a period during which the new lands were colonized. As these colonies grew and prospered, overseas trade was established that benefited both Europe and the colonies. New food sources were discovered. The extremely rich cod fishery of the Grand Banks became within sailing distance of European sailing vessels. The potato, a native of South America, was introduced into Europe by the Spanish in the sixteenth century and became one of the world's main food crops.

In addition to establishing long-range commerce and communications (other than the camel caravans that had been crossing the Asian deserts since ancient times), the sail played an important role in the outcome of international events. Alfred Thayer Mahan, in the preface to his *The Influence of Sea Power upon History, 1630–1783,* states that historians have vastly underestimated "the effect of sea power upon the course of history and the prosperity of nations" (vi). After the defeat of the Spanish Armada in 1588, England eventually became the dominant maritime nation, prevented the invasion of England by Napoleon's troops, and forced his ultimate defeat. All this was achieved through sea power, and the primary factor of sea power was the proficient use of sails.

This book traces the development of the art and science of sailing in Western civilization, which led eventually to the final adoption of the two classic sailing rigs: the square rig and the fore-and-aft rig. It must be understood, though, that sailing to windward probably originated earlier than it did in the West—in other civilizations whose peoples lived in other parts of the world.

Chronology

c. 6000 B.C.	Crude painting of sailing craft drawn on Egyptian vase; first documentary evidence of a sail.
c. 4700 B.C.	Egyptians develop reed hull; river sailing craft with square sail; mast located forward; can sail only downwind.
c. 3000 B.C.	Egyptians develop wood hull made of cedar imported from present-day Lebanon.
c. 1600 B.C.	Egyptians place mast in center of vessel and lower sail; can sail with the wind 45 degrees from stern.
c. 1500 B.C.	Cretans develop mast supported with stays; can sail across the wind.
c. 700 B.C.	Phoenicians develop long straight keel; can sail against the wind; first to build vessels without rowing ports.
c. 400 B.C.	Triangular lateen sail appears in Mediterranean; lateen has exceptional windward performance.
c. A.D. 800	Viking longships use single square sail and oars.
	Vikings optimize performance of square sail with *beitass* (temporary spar) inserted into luff of sail to improve sail's windward performance; later Vikings use beitass with bridle and bowline to improve sailing to windward.
1100s	Viking longship evolves into a larger ship, which would become the cog, with square sail and no oars.
c. 1180	Stern-mounted hinged rudder invented and applied to cog.
1200s	Beitass becomes a permanently attached spar and called the bowsprit.
	Two- and three-masted all-lateen vessels called caravels used throughout Mediterranean.

European cog with stern-mounted rudder, square-sail trimmed with bowline and bridle, and bowsprit sets scene for development of full-rigged ship.

1300s   Northern Europeans and Mediterraneans develop two-masted carrack with square sail and lateen steering sail.

1400s   Three-masted carrack is developed with square sails on foremast and mainmast, lateen sail on mizzenmast.

Dutch modify lateen sail to create fore-and-aft sprit rig.

1500s   Dutch invent jib sail.

Carrack evolves into three-masted galleon built with square sails, except for lateen sails on mizzen; considered to be first full-rigged ship and first man-of-war.

Spanish build high-charge galleon.

English build low-charge galleon, with best performance to windward.

1520   Gaff (spar to which head of fore-and-aft sail is attached) developed to create the fore-and-aft-gaff rig.

c. 1690   Wheel for steering developed.

1700s   East Indiaman, the best full-rigged merchantman, built.

1700   Fore-and-aft jibs and staysails applied to square riggers.

1713   First schooner built in America.

1750   Fore-and-aft spanker replaces lateen as a steering sail on square-riggers.

1751   Fast Baltimore clipper schooners built in Chesapeake Bay.

1761   Copper sheathing applied to ship's bottoms.

1794   United States Congress authorizes construction of six frigates.

1797   USS *Constitution* ("Old Ironsides") launched.

1818   Packets for transatlantic travel depart on fixed dates.

1832   *Ann McKimm* built, prototype of true clipper ship.

1837   Blackwall frigate (not a warship) built in Blackwall, England; proves faster than East Indiaman.

1845   *Rainbow*, first true clipper ship, built.

1847   Matthew Fontane Maury first publishes "Sailing Directions."

1850   Three-masted schooners built in America.

1851   Schooner yacht *America* built in New York; wins British Hundred Guinea Cup, which became the America's Cup.

1868   The clipper ship *Cutty Sark* launched (now on display in Greenwich, England).

1868	Suez Canal completed, ending era of the clipper ship.
1870	Spinnaker introduced on British racing yachts.
1880	Four-masted schooners built in America.
1882	Schooners equipped with steam winches and donkey boilers to raise sails and operate anchor windlass; require less crew.
1890	*Thomas W. Lawson,* a seven-masted schooner and the largest ever built; was lost in 1907.
	Cape Horners, square-riggers with steel hulls and steel rigging, built for the Chilean nitrate trade.
1916	Three-masted schooners constructed in United States for World War I.
1930	Square-riggers used in depression years (cheap labor); carry grain from Australia to Europe until World War II.
1942	The *Star of Scotland,* a schooner, sunk by German submarine.

To Harness the Wind

Egypt
and the
Early Mediterranean

The exact origin of the sail is still disputed by historians. Some contend that the sail was originated on the River Nile or evolved independently in Egypt and Indonesia.[1] Others believe that the sail existed earlier in the maritime island cultures, in Bahrain in the Arabian Gulf and in Malta in the Mediterranean.[2]

EGYPT

The earliest documentary evidence of a sailing craft is a crude painting on an Egyptian vase that dates back to 6000 B.C. A better description is provided by an Egyptian wall painting circa 4700 B.C. that shows a hull made of papyrus reed bundles (the boat in which the infant Moses was hidden on the bank of the Nile was also made of papyrus reeds). The bundles were lashed together to form an overhanging bow and stern. A fore-and-aft truss was required to raise the bow and stern. A single tall rectangular sail is mounted on an A-type mast as shown in figure 1; a conventional pole mast would have penetrated through the bottom of a reed hull.[3]

Figure 1. Egyptian reed hull sailing vessel, 4700 B.C., for sailing upstream and paddling downstream on the Nile.

The forward location of the mast permitted sailing only in a downwind direction (sailing ahead of the wind and probably a little to each side). An attempt to sail in any other direction would force the bow in a downwind direction. With the wind from any direction except astern, it was necessary to lower the sail and rely on paddles for propulsion. Sailing only downwind was satisfactory to the early Egyptians as the prevailing wind blew upstream on the Nile. They would sail upstream and for the return journey, take the sail down and paddle downstream with the current.[4]

By 3000 B.C. the reed hull was replaced with a wood hull made of cedar imported from present-day Lebanon.[5] The wood hull allowed the use of oars as the wood permitted the installation of a fulcrum (the pivot point support) required by an oar. A fulcrum was not feasible on a hull constructed of reeds. The fore-and-aft truss was retained. By 1600 B.C. the Egyptians centered the mast and made the sail lower and wider, but the mast was still without shrouds (side supports).[6] A lower yard was added to permit sheeting the sail to the still narrow hull (fig. 2). Lowering the sail reduced the heeling (leaning to the downwind side) effect and probably permitted sailing with a quartering wind (45 degrees from astern). A wind 50 degrees from the stern would be prohibitive because the spoon-shaped hull provided very little lateral resistance and the vessel would slide on the surface of the water in a downwind (leeward) direction.[7]

These vessels were seventy feet long, seventeen to eighteen feet wide; fully laden they had a draft of about three feet. They required fifteen oarsmen on

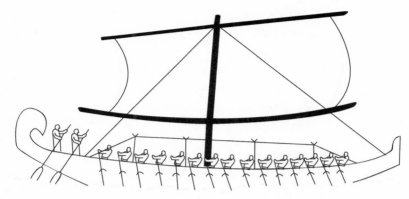

Figure 2. Egyptian wood hull sailing vessel, 1600 B.C. In vessels of this type the Egyptians sailed the Mediterranean and along the east coast of Africa.

each side and two or three steering oars on each side. The lower yard was supported by eight individual lines on each side of the mast as the sail cloth was not strong enough to support the weight of the lower yard. The halyards (ropes) that supported the lower yard were looped over a frame attached to the top of the mast and had to be hoisted against the friction of the frame, as the sheave or pulley was not yet invented.[8]

In these primitive vessels the Egyptians, in addition to sailing the Nile River, made remarkable ocean passages. The voyage to Syria, made as early as 2480 B.C., required paddling, and later rowing, as it was directly into the eye of the wind. Navigation consisted of following the coast on their right-hand side. The return trip was downwind and made under sail. Eventually the Egyptians voyaged to Crete, a distance of about four hundred miles, which required them to be out of sight of land for five or six days.[9]

From South Arabia and the African coast below the Red Sea, Egypt imported incense and other goods that came over land by countless small traders. To take over this trade Egypt built a port, with a ship-building capability, on the Red Sea. This formidable task was completed around 2000 B.C., as all materials required for construction of ships had to be transported about eighty-five kilometers, an eight-day journey across the desert.

The next step was to build a canal from the Nile to the Red Sea. At this time the Egyptians were already experienced canal builders. When branches of the Nile River began to silt up, they were excavated to form artificial canals for irrigation. As early as 2350–2170 B.C., the Egyptians dug a canal at the first cataract of the Nile to facilitate the movement of boats through the rapids.

The canal connecting the Nile to the Red Sea was initially completed in the twentieth century B.C. by the pharaoh Senusret. Although the route of the canal followed a gorge in the desert, construction was extremely difficult because the blowing sand tended to refill the excavation. Completion of the canal eliminated the caravan trips from the Red Sea to destinations in Egypt.

Later the canal was abandoned and allowed to silt up because Egypt was experiencing civil war troubles and parts of the country were ruled by foreign invaders. The canal was restored during the reign of Queen Hatshepsut (1479–1458), the first great woman ruler in history, and she reestablished commerce with the east coast of Africa for gold, ivory, ebony, incense, and even monkeys. The funerary temple of Queen Hatshepsut (on the bank of the Nile across the river from today's Thebes) includes three wall carvings of the Queen's ships of the type shown in figure 2, in the harbor of the land of Punt.[10] This ancient land was probably on the northern coast of present-day Somalia and perhaps farther south around the eastern tip of Africa.[11]

This basic sail of the Egyptians was ultimately adopted by the Phoenicians, Greeks, and Romans. It is believed that even the nations of the East learned shipbuilding from the Egyptians, who are justifiably credited with the establishment of the art of naval architecture.[12]

CRETE

Prior to 1450 B.C. the Cretans were the dominant sea power in the Mediterranean. The Egyptians referred to them as the "Sea People." The Cretans built rowing galleys and developed the ramming bow and built ramming galleys for the Greeks. With ships of this type, the Greeks defeated the Persians at the Battle of Salamis (480 B.C.) by destroying one half of the Persian fleet.[13]

The Cretans are also known as Minoans because of their mythical king Minos who, according to Greek mythology, ruled the Island of Crete where he created a trackless labyrinth and kept in it the Minotaur, a creature with the body of a man and the head of a bull.[14]

Unfortunately, documentation of the Minoan maritime accomplishments are not available as their civilization and the records of their achievements were destroyed by a tidal wave that followed a giant earthquake on a nearby island,[15] or by invaders from the north.[16] However, historians believe that the Minoans were the first to support the ship's masts with stays (front and back

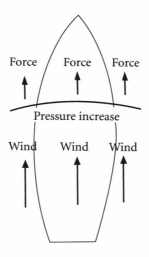

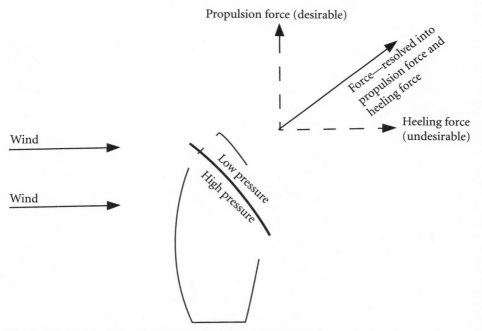

Figure 3. Sailing downwind. The sail converts the wind velocity into an increase in pressure on the windward side of the sail.

Figure 4. Sailing across the wind. The sail creates a slightly lower pressure on the leeward side of the sail and a slightly higher pressure on the windward side of the sail. The pressure difference acting against the area of the sail creates the propulsion force.

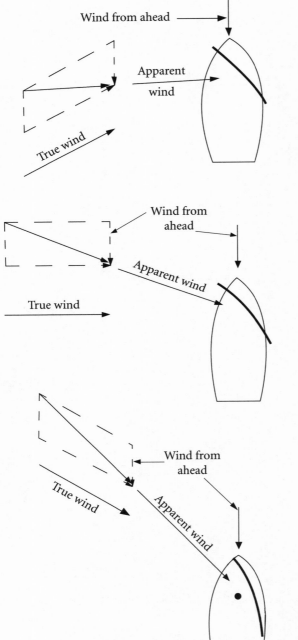

Wind from ahead

Apparent
wind

True wind

Figure 5. True wind from abaft the beam—apparent wind from the beam. The apparent wind is the resultant wind created by the true wind from the beam and the wind from ahead.

Wind from
ahead

Apparent wind

True wind

Figure 6. The true wind from the beam and the wind from ahead combine to create an apparent wind from forward of the beam.

Wind from
ahead

True wind

Apparent wind

Figure 7. Sailing against the true wind. The true wind from forward of the beam and the wind from ahead combine to form an apparent wind from ahead.

supports) and shrouds (side supports) and were the first to sail across the wind. Unfortunately, the historians do not specify if the Minoans sailed across the "true" wind or the "apparent" wind. Sailing across the true wind would have been more of an accomplishment.

Downwind sailing is rudimentary; the wind increases pressure on the upwind side of the sail, which in turn propels the vessel in the downwind direction (fig. 3). Sailing across the wind is significantly more complex and subjects the vessel to the danger of capsizing. The sail must be positioned so that its leading edge splits the oncoming wind (like the wing of an airplane) to create two separate wind streams, with the upwind (windward) air stream at a slightly greater pressure than the downwind (leeward) air stream. This difference in air pressure acting across the area of the sail produces (1) a propulsion force that moves the vessel in a forward direction and (2) a heeling (leeward)[17] force that slides the vessel along the surface of the water in a downwind direction and also heels (leans) the vessel, which creates the danger of capsizing (fig. 4). There are also two wind streams that combine to form an apparent (compromise) wind. One wind stream is the true wind created by nature and the other is created by the forward movement of the vessel. The compromise (resultant) wind is called the apparent wind—the wind that actually strikes the sail. The apparent wind is always from a direction forward of the true wind, except when the ship is sailing directly downwind. When the true wind is from abaft (astern of) the beam (the side of the vessel), the apparent wind approaches the beam (fig. 5); and when the true wind is from the beam, the apparent wind is from forward of the beam (fig. 6). Sailing against the true wind is more challenging yet because the apparent wind is more from the forward direction (fig. 7). The Minoans, who learned to reduce the heeling force by trimming (positioning) the sail, were probably the first to sail across the wind. The Phoenicians later perfected this technique and, after their development of the keel, were most likely the first to sail against the wind.

PHOENICIA

After 1450 B.C., the Phoenicians became the dominant sea power in the Mediterranean. They inherited the nautical knowledge of the Minoans and over a period of several hundred years, made many improvements. Some are still in use today. They deleted the long overhanging bow and stem originated by the Egyptians, provided life rails, built hulls with multiple decks and hatches, and invented the *deadeye* (fig. 8) used to tighten shrouds. They also invented the long straight keel, which increased the lateral resistance of the hull to permit sailing against the wind, and were the first to build ships without rowing ports.[18] The Phoenicians also established the basic concept of hull construction that remained in effect for centuries. The internal support structure of their ships consisted of a keel, and a stempost and sternpost attached to each end of the keel; fitted at intervals to the keel were frames (ribs) curved to the shape of the hull. The frames were also held in place by deck beams that ran laterally across each pair of frames. The side planking was attached to the edge of the frames, providing a rigid structure that held the ship together longitudinally, laterally, and vertically.[19]

The Phoenicians were the first to use stars to plot a course at night and knew that at local noon the sun was due south (a valid assumption as the Phoenicians voyaged north of the Equator; south of the Equator the sun is due north at local noon). Using stars for plotting was especially useful when combined with a navigational aid known as a Wind Rose, a circular card that displayed the direction of certain known winds. By lining up the north point on the card with the North Star or the south point to the sun at noon, the navigator could identify which wind was blowing and adjust his course accordingly.[20]

The Phoenicians' smaller vessel was the gallus and was mostly used for local trading. For longer voyages they developed a larger vessel, the hippo or Tarshis ship (fig. 9).[21] The site of the city of Tarshis has never been discovered, but it is believed to be somewhere on the Iberian peninsula, probably on the Atlantic coast of what is now Spain or Portugal.[22] *Hippo* was from *hippol* (horse's head). The horse's head was typically displayed on these vessels, sometimes on the bow and stern.[23] There were two types of Tarshis ships. The earlier type had a single square sail set between an upper and lower yard on a centered mast, a length to beam ratio of two and a half to one, a steering oar on each quarter, a full deck with two hatches, and stanchion and rails to protect the crew and to keep cargo from sliding overboard in rough weather. Cargo was stored above and below deck.

The other Tarshis ship was larger and had two masts. The forward mast was small and could be considered a high-sloping bowsprit. The larger mast was supported with shrouds (side supports) that were tensioned with deadeyes. There was no apparent provision for rowers.[24] The forward mast (the *aremon*) was located well forward and carried a small sail that, because of its forward location, permitted balancing the helm.[25] A single sail tends to turn a vessel in an upwind or downwind direction, and rudder action is

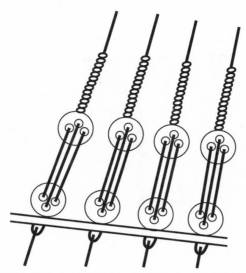

Figure 8. The Phoenician deadeye used to tighten shrouds. This method remained in use after the invention of the block.

required to steer a straight course. A steering oar was used at this time because the rudder had not yet been invented. With a single sail, a frequent movement of the steering oar was required to steer a straight course; this slowed down the vessel because a steering oar (or rudder) course correction acts like a break. The second sail, located forward, could be trimmed to off-set the turning tendency of the main sail and minimize the need for course corrections by the steering oar, which would have substantially improved sail performance.

The Tarshis ships voyaged to southern Britain and the Canary Islands, as well as sailing in the Mediterranean, the Red Sea, and the Indian Ocean. The canal from the Nile to the Red Sea provided access from the Mediterranean. The Phoenicians also were reputed to have circumnavigated Africa in 600 B.C. in an expedition instigated by Necho, a king of Egypt (610–594 B.C.), but the ships and all participants in the voyage were Phoenicians. They sailed south through the Red Sea, then along the east coast of Africa, rounded the south-ern tip of Africa (now the Cape of Good Hope), then north along the west coast of Africa and into the Mediterranean. When autumn came, they set-tled ashore, planted corn, and after harvesting it, they resumed their journey. Two years later they entered the Mediterranean and in the third year returned

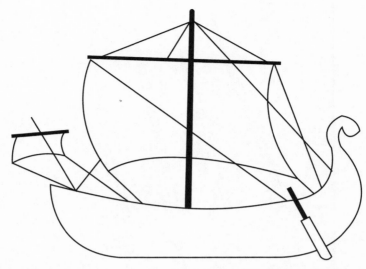

Figure 9. The Phoenician hippo or Tarshis ship. The small sail forward was used to offset the turning effect created by the large sail.

to Egypt, completing a fourteen-thousand-mile journey. The voyage was most probably made in large Tarshis ships because they were the most advanced vessels of the era and were equipped with a crow's nest at the masthead, which permitted a lookout to always keep the coastline in sight.[26] It was not until Europe's great Age of Discovery that a Portuguese fleet under Bartholomeu Dias managed to sail around Africa in A.D. 1491, a feat that the Phoenicians had achieved some two thousand years earlier in smaller ships with cruder sails and without the aid of a magnetic compass.

The Phoenicians' sea power in the Mediterranean and their proclivity for maritime advancement was suddenly terminated in 332 B.C., when Alexander the Great conquered the Phoenician city of Tyre.[27]

CARTHAGE AND THE PUNIC WARS

In addition to being mariners and traders, the Phoenicians were colonists. They established colonies in Sicily, Sardinia, Corsica, the Iberian Peninsula (today's Spain and Portugal), and Carthage (founded in about 750 B.C.), their major colony in North Africa near the present site of Tunis. After the defeat of the Phoenicians by Alexander the Great, Carthage became the leader of the other Phoenician colonies and was the dominant sea power in the western Mediterranean.

The First Punic War (264–241 B.C., Punic was the Roman word for Phoenician) resulted when the Romans sought to expel the Carthaginian invaders from eastern Sicily. Rome excelled in land warfare, but the Carthaginians were dominant at sea. With their war galleys built for speed under oars to facilitate ramming— the sail and even the mast were removed prior to combat and preferably stored ashore[28]—they defeated the Romans at sea until 260 B.C., when the Romans invented the *corvus* (raven), a gangplank thirty-six feet long and four feet wide with a heavy spike at one end. The spiked end of the gangplank was projected over the bow and when the Roman ship came close enough to the enemy vessel, the gangplank was dropped to embed the spike in the enemy's deck. As soon as the raven landed, eighty first-line Roman legionnaires would charge across the gangway to engage the enemy.

The Romans' corvus was a huge success; when the Romans first used it in a battle off the coast of Sicily, the Carthaginians lost forty-four ships. As the war progressed, the Romans built faster and more maneuverable ships by copying a captured Carthaginian vessel; the Romans also learned ramming tactics from their enemy. After twenty-three years of war, Carthage became distracted by revolts in her African possessions. Hampered by old ships with raw crews, the Carthaginians were finally defeated by the Romans, who had a superior number of newer ships manned by experienced crews.[29]

The Second Punic War (218–201 B.C.), instigated by the Carthaginians, was a land war. Because the Romans were still dominant at sea in the western Mediterranean, Hannibal, the famous Carthaginian general, was forced to march (with his elephants) the long perilous land route from Spain, through Gaul, and across the Alps into Italy. Yet, throughout the war, Roman legions were transported by water unmolested between Italy and Spain to intercept Hannibal's communications and to permit Scipio, the Roman general, to invade Spain and defeat nearly all of the Carthaginian subordinate generals. Hannibal was joined by the Gauls, traditional enemies of Rome, and campaigned successfully in Italy for fifteen years. He was to be reinforced by a support expedition led by his brother, Hasdrubal, who was also forced to take the land route through Gaul due to dominant Roman sea power. Before Hasdrubal could join up with Hannibal in southern Italy, the Romans rapidly shifted troops and defeated Hasdrubal in northern Italy. The defeat of this support expedition deprived Hannibal of reinforcements and victory there.[30] The Second Punic War, although a land campaign, is an important event in maritime history because it is probably the earliest major land warfare campaign that was contingent on the control of the sea (the second such incident was the mastery of the sea by the English that ultimately led to the defeat of Napoleon).[31]

The Romans were victorious in the Third (and last) Punic War (149–146 B.C.). They invaded Carthage and completely destroyed the Carthaginian civilization.

GREECE AND ROME

After the decline of the Phoenician maritime influence, the Mediterraneans made no significant voyages into the Atlantic until the end of the thirteenth century A.D. because the Greeks and Romans were primarily interested in warships. The Greeks were the first to make navigation into an art. They were the earliest mapmakers and astronomers and produced rough sea charts as early as the sixth century B.C.[32] Neither the Greeks nor the Romans made any major improvements to sailing technology, but the Romans did add a third mast and triangular sails above the square mainsail[33] and developed brails (a line passing through rings attached to the sail) by which a sail could be gathered to reduce sail area.[34] This configuration appeared in the first and second centuries A.D. on big merchant ships that the Romans built to haul grain from Egypt. These were very large ships; the largest was 180 feet long, 45 feet wide, and 44 feet deep in the hold. They were equipped with three masts with a square sail on each mast and two triangular top sails above the yard on the mainmast. The Romans had about one hundred grain ships in service at all times. It was centuries before a merchant fleet of comparable size came into being.[35]

BYZANTIUM

After the fall of Rome (A.D. 410) Byzantium was the dominant sea power in the eastern Mediterranean. The Byzantines made no significant advancements in sail technology, but they developed plank-on-frame construction for building the hull of a ship. Prior to this development, the sides of the hull were built first and then the reinforcing ribs, beams, and other structural members were added. The plank-on-frame method reversed that procedure. The internal frame was constructed first and then mounted on the keel. The outside planks were then attached to the frame. This method of hull construction is used to the present day.[36]

The
Lateen Sail

The Egyptian square sail remained in use in the Mediterranean until the lateen sail appeared sometime between the fourth century B.C.[1] and the first century A.D.[2] The lateen was a major breakthrough in the art of sailing because it permitted faster and closer sailing to windward. This sail is shaped like a triangle and suspended from a long diagonal yard (fig. 10). Use of the lateen sail spread with the advance of the Moslem culture (primarily in the eighth century A.D.) and then to the entire Mediterranean and the Black Sea.[3]

PERFORMANCE

The long diagonal yard of the lateen permitted positioning the leading edge (the luff) of the sail much closer to the vessel's fore-and-aft (front to back) centerline than was possible with the Egyptian square sail, and this permitted sailing closer to the direction from which the wind was blowing (higher pointing). The long yard also provided a long luff and consequently a large adjacent luff area, and the triangular shape of the sail resulted in a relatively small area for the trailing edge of the sail, called the *leech* area. To a great

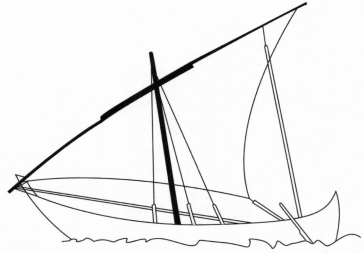

Figure 10. The lateen sail. Shrouds only on the windward side made tacking difficult, but the exceptional windward performance offset the tacking disadvantage.

extent, speed to windward depends on the sail's luff length; today's *high aspect ratio* sails have a long luff for greater speed to windward (fig. 11).

The force generated by a sail is actually the (vector) sum of all of the incremental forces acting on the entire area of the sail. Due to the curved surface of the sail (caused by the pressure of the apparent wind) the luff area produces the desirable propulsion forces and the leech area the undesirable heeling forces (fig. 12).[4] Thus, the lateen sail, because of its large luff area and small leech area, allows the vessel to sail fast to windward and with minimum heel. Excessive heeling is undesirable because it reduces the effective sail area and keel depth. Minimal heeling permitted the installation of a larger sail to obtain a still greater speed to windward without excessive heeling. (Some twentieth-century racing yachts were built with a long bow and stern overhang. When they heeled, the water line length was increased. As the maximum speed of a displacement hull increases with an increase in water line length, excessive heel on yachts of this design was an advantage.)

TACKING AND JIBING

The lateen rig did, however, have two major disadvantages. First, it made tacking difficult and required a large crew. Tacking is changing the direction of

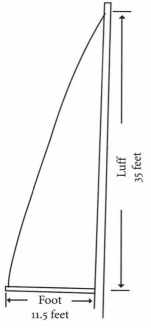

Figure 11. The aspect ratio of a modern sail. The long luff on this sail improves performance to windward.

Luff
35 feet

Foot
11.5 feet

Aspect ratio = luff/foot = 35/11.5 = 3.04

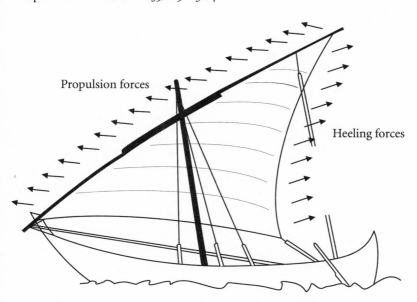

Propulsion forces

Heeling forces

Figure 12. Incremental forces on the lateen sail. The long luff provides mainly propulsion forces, and the short leach minimizes the heeling forces.

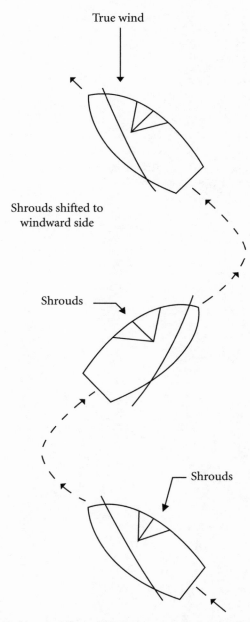

True wind

Shrouds shifted to
windward side

Shrouds

Shrouds

Figure 13. Tacking the lateen sail. The complexity of shifting the shrouds necessitated a large crew.

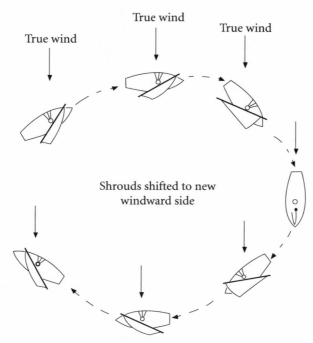

True wind

True wind

True wind

Shrouds shifted to new
windward side

Figure 14. To jibe, or wear ship, the lateen sail. Jibing is a less complicated maneuver than tacking; the wind from astern billows the sail forward and away from the mast, making it easier to shift the sail and yard to the opposite side of the mast.

a vessel so that its bow passes through the direction of the true wind (fig. 13). The mast on the lateen rig was supported with only one set of shrouds (side supports) located on the windward side. If the mast had shrouds on both sides, the leeward shrouds would interfere with the diagonal yard. Tacking required (1) placing the diagonal yard into a vertical position, (2) moving the yard and sail to the opposite side of the mast, and (3) restoring the yard to its original diagonal orientation. During this complex evolution, other crew members shifted the mast support shrouds to the opposite (the new windward) side. Instead of tacking with the lateen sail, *wear ship* (jibing) was the preferred maneuver. Wear ship is the opposite of tacking; the vessel is turned so that its stern passes through the direction of the true wind. When the ship turns in the downwind direction, the wind from astern billows out the sail and forces the yard into a vertical position. As the turn continues, the yard and sail swivel to the other side of the mast (fig. 14).[5] Second, shortening the lateen sail's area (reefing) was a complex and time-consuming task because it had no reef points.[6] To shorten the sail area, the yard had to be dropped, the sail detached from the yard, a smaller sail attached, and the yard and sail hoisted again.

Nevertheless, because of its high pointing ability and speed to windward, the lateen proved to be the ideal sail for the usually calm waters and shifting winds of the Mediterranean. A two- and three-masted vessel equipped with lateen sails was eventually called a caravel (fig. 15) and the rowing war galley, a galleass (fig. 16).

ORIGIN

Historians disagree about the origin of the lateen, which remains a mystery. Some historians believe it to have originated in present-day Indonesia; a sail of similar triangular shape was used in the proa, a boat (usually without a deck) of the Pacific Islands.[7] Then again the lateen may have first been used in India, after which it spread into the Pacific and into the Mediterranean. Some argue that it was invented by Arabs in the East and

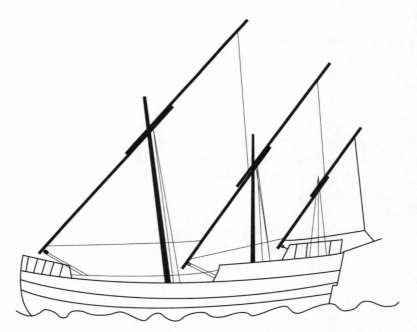

Figure 15. The caravel—with lateen sails. These vessels were used at the onset of the Age of Discovery by the Portuguese to explore the northwest coast of Africa.

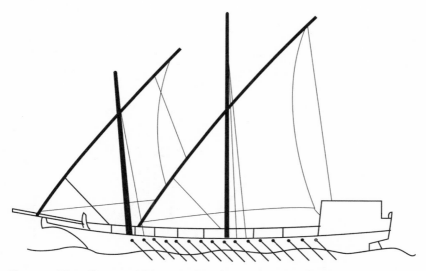

Figure 16. The galleass—with lateen sails and oars. These vessels were a compromise between the caravel and the oared galley.

later introduced into the Mediterranean, but others contend that the development in the East was completely independent of the Arab development in the Mediterranean.[8]

One popular theory is that the lateen sail may have been adapted from the original Egyptian square sail. The Egyptian nugger sail (fig. 17) was probably an intermediate stage of development and consisted of tilting the yards of the square sail. The next stage was the deletion of the lower yard and extending the upper yard to obtain the long, rigid luff that gave the lateen its exceptional performance to windward. The nugger sail was still in use on the Nile above the second cataract in the early 1900s.[9]

Another theory holds that the lateen originated from the use of brails on the Egyptian square sail. When sailing to windward in a strong wind, the brails aft of the mast could be selectively tightened to reduce the sail area aft of the mast and minimize the vessel's tendency to turn into the wind (round up). Tightening the brails in this manner converted the sail into a triangular shape. By tightening the luff and slacking the leech, the yard would be forced into a diagonal position to form the basic geometry of the lateen. The original vertical luff of the square sail would form the horizontal foot of the lateen and the selectively tightened brails would form the leech.[10]

Figure 17. The Egyptian nugger. This sail may have been the forerunner of the lateen sail and remained in use on the upper Nile as late as the early twentieth century.

The most plausible explanation for the origin of the Mediterranean lateen is that it evolved from the settee sail, also known as the Arabian lateen, used on the dhows of the east coast of Africa and the Indian Ocean.[11] More than three thousand years before the birth of Christ, commerce existed between India and Babylon, at the head of the Persian Gulf, and Arab, Persian, and Indian seagoing dhows have sailed the Indian Ocean "from time immemorial." The assumption that the lateen evolved from the settee has to do with the two monsoons in the Indian Ocean (*monsoon* is Arabic for season): the wind blows from the northeast from October to April and from the southwest from May to October. It would seem logical to assume that vessels equipped with the Egyptian square sail could sail—basically downwind—across the Indian Ocean in one season and return, again sailing downwind, in the other season. This, however, was not feasible because the early Egyptian craft, with their square sails, could not have survived during the extremely stormy southwest wind season.[12]

The northeast monsoon is actually part of the northeast trade wind from the Pacific Ocean, but when the sun moves north of the equator, it heats the landmass of southeast Asia and nullifies the effect of the trade wind, allowing the stormy winds from the southwest into the Indian Ocean. These fierce winds, accompanied by heavy rain that could last for forty or fifty days, create high stormy seas; even steamships have typically sought shelter in a protected port during this stormy monsoon.[13] So the ancient mariners had to sail in both directions during the favorable northwest wind monsoon. Because the Egyptian square sail could not carry a vessel against the wind, an improved sail was required, and the settee sail fulfilled this need. The settee is similar in shape and operation to the Mediterranean lateen but with the front corner cut off making it four-sided (fig. 18). It sailed well to windward and, of course, could sail downwind. The settee resembles the Chinese junk sail that also sails well to windward.

TWENTIETH CENTURY

The lateen is a high-performance sail, capable of sailing within about 56.25 degrees of the true wind.[14] It has been in continuous use for over two thousand years and is the forerunner of today's fore-and-aft sail. For the Nile a vessel called the *ghayassah* was developed with an elongated lateen, tall enough

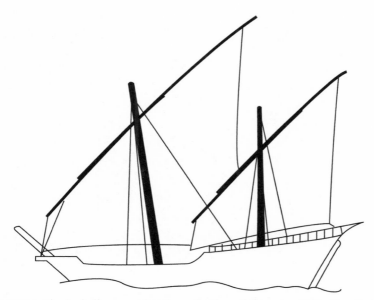

Figure 18. The Arab dhow—with settee sails. The sail shape resembles the sail of the Chinese junk. The settee is the most probable forerunner of the lateen sail.

to extend above the obstructing banks and catch the wind.[15] The primitive Arab dhow, equipped with lateen or settee sails, was used well into the twentieth century for carrying dates and sometimes passengers along the east coast of North Africa. Alan Villiers, one of the last square-rig captains and renowned maritime author described his 1938 voyage in a small dhow. He writes, "She had no lights, no charts, no log, no log line, no anchor save a grapnel and a handy piece of stone—the little dhow—sailed like a bird and the lateen sail pulled beautifully."[16]

3

The
Viking
Contribution

According to Norse legend, the Scandinavians migrated in 3000 B.C. from the Black Sea area, up the Russian rivers, and then overland to the Baltic.[1] Their first vessels were dugouts, and later vessels were made of hides stretched over curved wooden frames. The Scandinavians, sea warriors and raiders who became known as Vikings (from the Old Norse word *vikingr,* the practice of marauding or piracy), ventured into the open sea about A.D. 750 and then made rapid strides in the art of sailing. They probably learned to sail from the Frisians, who learned from the Gauls, who in turn may have learned from the Veneti of Brittany, who battled against Caesar in 56 B.C. with vessels equipped with sails of leather.[2] The Vikings raided into England, France, and Northern Spain and eventually the basic design of the Norse sail extended from the North Cape to the Bay of Biscay[3] and remained in use for the next four hundred years.[4] The word *sail* is from the Old Norse word *sigla.*[5]

The Vikings also voyaged to Iceland and Greenland from today's Norway and to the Western Hemisphere about five hundred years before Columbus. Erik the Red established a colony in Greenland in A.D. 985, and one of his followers, Biarni Heriulfsson, was blown off course on a voyage to Greenland and sighted land to the west of Greenland. Leif Eriksson, the son of Erik the

Red, followed Heriulfsson's route and discovered what is now believed to be Baffin Island, Labrador, and Newfoundland.[6]

Like other mariners of that era, the Vikings' preferred method of navigation was to use landmarks. In sailing from Norway to Iceland and to Greenland, they used sightings on the Shetland and Faeroe Islands. The Vikings also took sightings of the sun and stars to determine direction and to approximate their position. By the late tenth century they developed a system that approximated latitude. They formulated a table of figures that showed the sun's midday height for each week of the year. By using a notched measuring stick and the table of the sun's height, they were able to estimate their latitude.[7]

To determine the direction of the closest land, they used ravens. These birds, known for their ability to find land, were carried on board and when it was necessary to determine the course toward land, one would be released and the Vikings would sail in the same direction that the raven was flying. The raven became the Vikings' favorite symbol and was displayed on their flag.[8] The practice of releasing ravens was continued into the eighteenth century and this led to the term crow's nest for the small shelter on the foremast for the masthead lookout.

THE LONGSHIP

Used for war, the Viking longship (fig. 19), measured 90 to 120 feet in length (cargo ships were shorter). She was light and fast, with a shallow draft that permitted beaching, and propelled by oars and a single square sail suspended from a horizontal yard attached to a single centrally located mast. The mast was supported by two shrouds, a forestay, and a backstay. Braces were attached to each end of the yard and consisted of a block and tackle arrangement; the sheets and halyards were led to a wooden windlass located aft near the stern.[9]

The longship was steered by a device located aft on the starboard side that had been referred to as a steering board and sometimes as a steering oar. Using the term *oar* for *board*, however, is something of a misnomer. An oar is attached to the hull at a single point; to change the direction in which the vessel is heading, the blade of the steering oar is moved away from the hull, creating a resistance that turns the vessel to that side. This was the method used by the early Mediterraneans; one or more steering oars were located at each side near the stern. A centrally located steering oar changes the vessel's direction in the same manner and can also be used to row the stern in the direction opposite of the

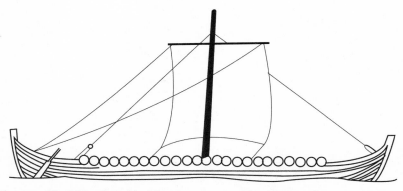

Figure 19. The Viking longship. The Norsemen used longships as their war vessels. It was customary for them to place their shields on the gunwales prior to entering battle.

desired turn; during the eighteenth, nineteenth, and twentieth centuries, the latter method was used in whaleboats when under oars.

Unlike the steering oar, the Viking steering board, or steerboard, was attached to the hull at two points and was rotated around a vertical axis to obtain water resistance against the elongated blade that turned the vessel.[10] Because this device could be rotated in either direction, it could instigate a turn to port or to starboard without another steering board on the opposite side (fig. 20). A horizontal arm, a tiller, was attached to the top of the board to facilitate rotating the submerged blade. Steerboard is the origin of today's starboard as that is the side on which the steerboard was mounted. In port, the opposite side of the vessel was placed alongside the dock or quay to prevent damage to the steerboard. The side along the quay was equipped with a load board to facilitate handling cargo, and this side was called the larboard side. However, when the wind was up, starboard could be confused with larboard, so the name of the left side of the vessel was changed to *port* since it was that side of the vessel that was alongside the dock or quay when in port.[11]

WINDWARD PERFORMANCE

The Vikings' major contribution to the technology of sailing was to optimize the windward performance of the square sail. The square sail is not well suited for sailing against the wind; it cannot readily be positioned close to the fore-and-aft centerline of the vessel, and the unsupported vertical leading edge (the

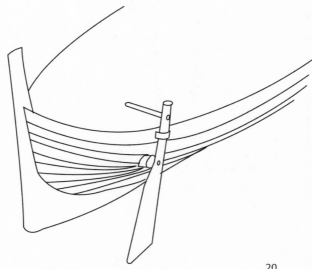

Figure 20. The Viking steerboard. The steerboard pivoted about a vertical axis and was the forerunner of the rudder.

luff) of the sail tends to curl back toward the center of the sail; a wind from further astern is required to fill the sail.

The Vikings employed the beitass, a temporary spar (like today's whisker pole), to minimize the curl of the leech.[12] One end of the beitass was inserted into a fitting attached to the luff of the sail and the other end was positioned near the base of the mast. This minimized the curl of the luff and also pushed the luff of the sail to windward allowing the vessel to sail closer to the direction from which the wind was blowing (fig. 21). An alternate arrangement was to position the end of the beitass ahead of the sail and, with a bowline and a bridle, pull the windward edge of the sail forward. This also minimized the curl in the luff and allowed a closer course to windward (fig. 22). Both of these rigging arrangements were major improvements in trimming the square sail for sailing to windward and remained in use for centuries. The beitass-inserted-into-the-luff method was used on the fast French *chasse-marée* (sea chaser) luggers as late as the seventeenth and eighteenth centuries; and the bowline and bridle method was still in use on the nineteenth-century clipper ships.

The excellent windward performance of the Viking square-sail arrangement was confirmed in 1893 when a replica of a Viking longship crossed the

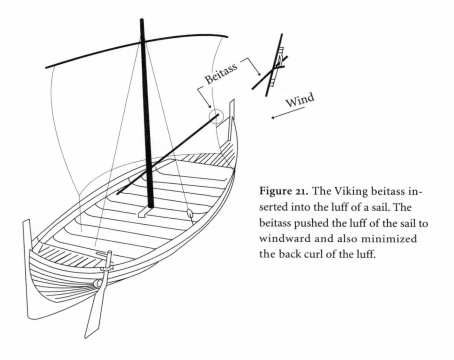

Figure 21. The Viking beitass inserted into the luff of a sail. The beitass pushed the luff of the sail to windward and also minimized the back curl of the luff.

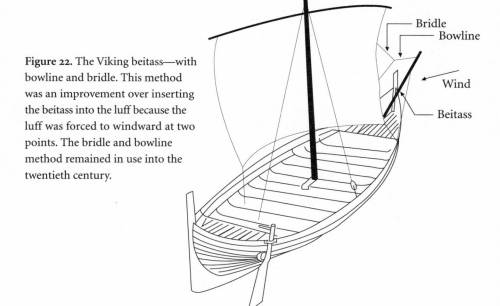

Figure 22. The Viking beitass—with bowline and bridle. This method was an improvement over inserting the beitass into the luff because the luff was forced to windward at two points. The bridle and bowline method remained in use into the twentieth century.

Atlantic in twenty-eight days averaging a hundred miles per day[13] on a course that was mostly to windward, against the prevailing northwest winds of the North Atlantic. The Viking longship design and sail arrangement was adopted throughout Europe and remained in use through the eleventh century. The famous Bayeux Tapestry depicting William the Conqueror's invasion of England in 1066 shows that his ships were the standard Viking-style long-ships.[14] William the Norman and the settlers of Normandy were of Norse/Viking heritage, so it was natural for them to use such vessels.

THE COG

By 1100, the Viking longship had evolved into a larger vessel, called a cog, which is illustrated in figure 23. The cog was also known as a roundship because of its short length-to-beam ratio.[15] The cog was still equipped with the single Viking square sail but featured a massive mast that supported a platform. Platforms were also located at the bow and stern to accommo-date archers shooting down on the crewmen of enemy ships. By 1300 these platforms, or castles, grew in size and were the origin of today's forecastle (pronounced fo'c'sle), the space below the short raised deck at the bow that during the Age of Sail became the crew's quarters. Also at some time dur-ing the 1200s, the beitass became a permanently attached spar and was called a bowsprit.[16] Its sole purpose was to provide a forward lead point to allow the bowline, attached to the windward side of the sail by means of a bridle, to pull the windward side of the sail forward to permit sailing closer to the wind.

The most significant development on the cog was the stern-mounted hinged rudder (fig. 23) that was first used about 1180.[17] The rudder was far more effective for steering a vessel than the Viking-developed steerboard located aft on the right side. When the vessel was heeled to port, steering was difficult because the steerboard would tend to lift out of the water.[18] The stern-mounted hinged rudder permitted more precise steering, and this vastly improved sail performance and consequently minimized the need for oars.

The cog was the work ship of Europe from 1100 to 1400 and was partic-ularly popular with the Hanseatic League, originally a maritime trading confederation of German towns. The Hanseatic League started in about 1240 and reached its height in trading activity in northwestern Europe in the fourteenth and early fifteenth centuries. It was actively involved in the development of ships.[19] The Hansa cog was a hundred feet long and twenty-five feet wide; it had a draft of ten feet and a single large square sail of two thousand square feet.[20] But it was the invention of the stern-mounted hinged rudder and the bowsprit that transformed the basic Viking longship design into a true ship and set the stage for the development of the full-rigged ship.

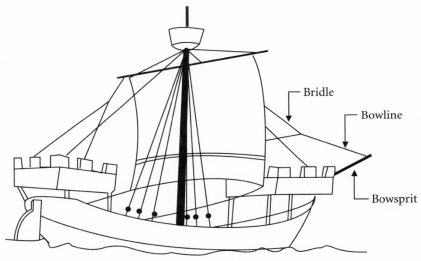

Bridle

Bowline

Bowsprit

Figure 23. The European cog—with stern-mounted rudder, bowsprit, bowline, and bridle. The sole purpose of the bowsprit was to provide a forward lead point for the bowline, which exerted tension on the bridle.

The
Full-Rigged
Ship

The Third Crusade in A.D. 1268 began, among other things, nautical cultural exchanges. Northern Europeans sailed into the Mediterranean and learned about multiple masts and the exceptional windward performance of the lateen sail (the Europeans named the sail lateen because it was used in Latin countries). The Mediterraneans, in turn, were impressed with the northern European stern-mounted, hinged rudder and the bowsprit that improved the windward performance of the square sail.[1] Ready to venture into the Atlantic, the Mediterraneans realized that although the lateen was ideal for the light, shifting winds of the Mediterranean, the square sail was best for the Atlantic's strong and steady trade winds.

THE CARRACK

In the early 1300s the single-masted cog was equipped with a small lateen sail aft, and this type of vessel became known as a carrack (fig. 24).[2] Later, large carracks were equipped with three masts with square sails on the foremast and mainmast, and a lateen on the after (mizzen) mast. Because the lateen could be trimmed closer to the wind, it was used to balance the helm and became

Figure 24. An early two-masted carrack. In the early 1300s the Viking square sail was used with a Mediterranean lateen.

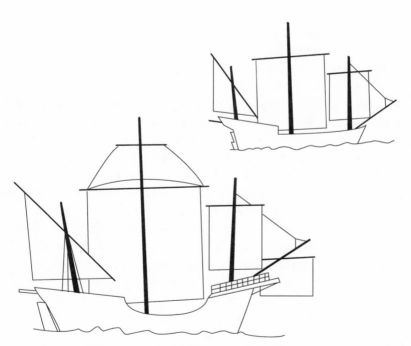

Figure 25. Three-masted carracks. Early carracks *(above)* had one sail on each mast. Later carracks were equipped with a topsail on the mainmast and a spritsail under the bowsprit.

known as a steering sail.[3] Later still, a top (square) sail was added to the main-mast and another square sail was located under the bowsprit (fig. 25). Some of the larger carracks were equipped with an additional lateen mounted on a fourth mast, called the bonaventure, and located aft of the mizzenmast; the lateen mizzen was a drive (propulsion) sail and the bonaventure lateen was the steering sail.[4]

The square sails on the carrack provided a much larger sail area than the all-lateen caravel, and this made the carrack a much faster vessel when the wind was from astern to slightly forward of the beam. Square sails also per-mitted a much smaller crew.[5] The complex tacking procedure required for lateens was eliminated, except for the small lateen steering sail, and square sails could be reefed much more easily than lateens.

The carrack proved to be an exceptionally seaworthy vessel because of its high freeboard (the vertical extension of the hull above the water line) aft, which also acted as a sail area. In stormy weather, all sails would be taken down, the helm lashed, so that the entire crew could go below. Since the high freeboard aft provided a greater sail area than the lower freeboard forward, the wind would force the stern downwind, turning the bow into the wind and usually the oncoming waves. In this manner the carrack could ride out the severest storms.

Historians have sometimes mistaken carracks for caravels. This confusion stems from the Mediterranean sailors' adoption of square sails. Before the northern Europeans arrived in the Mediterranean in the thirteenth century, the Mediterranean vessels had only lateen sails and the commercial vessels were called caravels, as shown in figure 15, chapter 2. After the introduction of the Viking-type square sails, the all-lateen ships were called caravel latinas, and those equipped with square sails on the foremast and mainmast were called caravel redondas (or *caravela latinas* and *caravela rotundas*).[6] The square sails of a caravel *redonda* (round) gave the vessel a more rounded appearance than that of a caravel latina with its triangular lateen sails.

Before his first voyage, Columbus equipped the caravel *Pinta* with square sails, making it a caravel redonda, and converted the *Niña* to square sails in the Canaries because she was a particularly slow sailer in the Atlantic trade winds. Most historians believe that Columbus's largest ship, the *Santa Maria* was a true carrack; although some classify it as a caravel redonda. The major difference was that the carrack had a low bow platform and the bowsprit was to starboard of the stem.[7] Columbus's ships were also referred to as *naos* (sin-gular, *nao*), the Spanish word for ships in that era, but *nao* did not specify the arrangement of the sails, or the sail plan.[8] The difference in terminology is not of prime importance because the carrack and the caravel redonda had basically the same sail plan. The significant issue is that this sail arrangement, square sails on two masts and a steering sail on the mizzen, became the fundamental sail plan for the full-rigged ship.

VOYAGES OF DISCOVERY

Virtually all the extensive voyages of discovery were made in carracks. The Portuguese voyages were instigated by Prince Henry of Portugal (1394–1460), although the most significant Portuguese voyages were made after his death. Prince Henry distinguished himself in military action against the Moors, who threatened to engulf Europe with the spread of Islam. The wealth of the Islamic world was based on control of the sea routes in the Indian Ocean.[9] Spices (to preserve food), jewels, silk, ivory, and other goods desired by Mediterraneans and northern Europeans were imported from India, the Malay Peninsula, and even China.[10] This was the route that had been controlled by the Arabs long before the birth of Christ. The other trade route was from China and was the overland Silk Road through central China, the Black Sea, and Syria.

Prince Henry, who became known as Prince Henry the Navigator, knew of the purported circumnavigation of Africa by the Phoenicians for the Egyptian king Necho, and he theorized that if he could establish a sea route around Africa connecting Portugal to the East, he would diminish the power of the Islamic world at its source. To implement his plan, he assembled mathematicians, astronomers, navigators, cartographers and practical seamen to convert Portugal's coastal fishermen into educated mariners capable of conducting extensive exploratory voyages. In effect, he created the science of navigation.[11]

The first voyages to explore the west coast of Africa were made in the all-lateen caravels; these were small vessels ideal for inshore exploration because of their shallow draft, and they sailed well to windward. After rounding the Capo De Nao, the western bulge of Africa, the Portuguese shifted to sailing carracks for better performance in the trade winds. By this time they had gained sufficient confidence in sailing to windward with square sails equipped with bowlines and bridles.[12]

The Portuguese mariner Bartholomeu Dias (c. 1450–1500) explored the coast of Africa and in 1488 became the first European to sail around the continent's southern tip, which he named the Cape of Storms. On his return, however, the name was changed to Cape of Good Hope, probably to prevent future mariners from fearing to sail there. In a subsequent voyage to this area, Dias's ship foundered in a storm, and, ironically, he perished at his Cape of Storms.[13]

Vasco da Gama (1460–1524) made the first voyage to India in 1497.[14] After entering the Indian Ocean, he demonstrated the versatility of the carrack by shifting from square sails to the more weatherly lateen sails,[15] which indicates that he must have encountered the northeast monsoon. Subsequent voyages by Vasco da Gama finally established trade factories in the East.

Prince Henry the Navigator died in 1460, but his dream was realized. The Portuguese completed taking over the East Indies trade from the Arabs in 1540.[16]

THE FIFTEENTH CENTURY

Ships became much larger during the fifteenth century. Originally trade with China and India was overland to the Levant, then through Venice and into the cities of Europe. In the fifteenth century trade expanded, and there was an incentive to ship cargo directly from the Levant into European ports. The original astronomic work of the Egyptians was verified and the first tables of the sun's declination were published in 1478. The German astronomer, Martin Behem (c. 1435–1507), constructed the first globe to show that the Earth was round. The magnetic compass had arrived in Europe in about 1400.[17]

In order to carry goods safely, ships needed a means to protect themselves primarily from coastal pirates. And for this, gunpowder became available. Gunpowder was first used aboard ships in about 1335; but it wasn't until 1513 that the first ship was sunk by gunfire.[18] As guns became larger and heavier, larger ships were required to carry them. The nautical world was now ready for global voyages. Ships had to be built larger so that they could carry more cargo, armament, food, and water for longer voyages. By the end of the fifteenth century, ships were four times larger than at the start of that century.[19]

THE GALLEON

The galleon, not to be confused with the oar-powered galley, was a larger ship that evolved from the carrack.[20] The Old Spanish word *galéon* is a source for galleon, although the name of the vessel may have come from the Italian *galleoni*. The sail plan was basically the same as the carrack's, but taller masts permitted installation of more topsails. Some carried a lateen topsail above the mizzen lateen and an additional lateen, on a fourth mast, the bonaventure.

Magellan supposedly first circumnavigated the Earth in 1520 in his carrack, the *Trinidad*, but he actually started his 1519 voyage with five ships; only the *Trinidad* and the *Vittoria* reached the Philippines, where Magellan was killed. Later, the *Trinidad*, leaky and undermanned, was abandoned, and it was the *Vittoria*, under Juan Sebastián del Cano, that first circumnavigated the Earth.[21]

Sir Francis Drake's 1577 circumnavigation, the second, was in his galleon, originally called the *Pelican* but renamed the *Golden Hind* during the voyage. It was during this voyage that Drake discovered Cape Horn, but he did not sail around the Cape from the Atlantic to the Pacific. He sailed through the Straits of Magellan, but on entering the Pacific, he encountered a severe and lengthy storm that drove his ship in a southeasterly direction, permitting Drake to discover the southernmost point of South America.[22] Cape Horn was first rounded in 1616 by Jakob le Maire. He named it Cape Hoorn after the town in which he was born, a small seaport in North Holland.[23]

Upon his return to England, 26 September 1580, Drake was knighted by Queen Elizabeth and the *Golden Hind* was towed into a small creek near the royal dockyard in Deptford and walled in with earth, to serve as a memorial. Over the years the memorial went to ruin; future archaeologists may someday uncover the hull of one of the most famous ships of all time. A replica of the *Golden Hind* was constructed in 1974. Recently discovered documents revealed that there were some dimensional inaccuracies in the construction of the replica, but she sailed twice around the world and is presently on display in London. The latest documents indicate that the original *Golden Hind* was 150 tons, approximately eighty feet between stem and sternpost, a beam of twenty-three feet, and a keel about two and a half times as long as her beam.[24]

WARSHIPS

The Spanish built large galleons. Seven- and eight-hundred-ton ships were common, and some ships weighed as much as a thousand tons.[25] These large ships were used to make annual trips from Manila in the Philippines to Acapulco in Mexico, making a landfall in California. Manila was founded by the Spanish in 1571; it became the collection point of treasures and other rich cargo that were shipped to Spain by way of Mexico.[26] It was the capture of the Spanish treasure galleon, *Nuestra Señora de la Concepción*, by Sir Francis Drake (1579) that provided his greatest haul and more than paid for his entire

Figure 26. The high-charge galleon. The high structure forward impeded sailing to windward.

voyage.[27] These large Spanish galleons became known as high-charge galleons because of their high freeboard, both forward and aft, shown in figure 26. The high freeboard provided better protection; it made boarding more difficult. The high freeboard also made these ships clumsy sailors, however, especially in rough seas.

When war between Spain and England seemed imminent, Sir John Hawkins designed ships for Elizabeth's navy that became known as low-charge galleons, which are shown in figure 27. Hawkins had made several voyages around Africa and to the West Indies in vessels of the original high-charge design and discovered that the high freeboard forward caught the wind and forced the bow in a downwind direction. This made it extremely difficult—and in a strong wind even impossible—for a vessel to hold her course to windward. In 1570 Hawkins experimented with vessels that did not have the extremely high forecastle superstructure, making them much more maneuverable and weatherly. He also implemented a Dutch invention that permitted detaching and lowering topmasts in exceptionally stormy weather. Initially, topmasts were fixed spars permanently attached to the lower mast, and in rough weather their weight aloft could create a dangerous condition.[28]

Lowering topmasts became a common practice for vessels preparing to round Cape Horn where stormy weather could be expected.

For the low-charge design, he also changed the length-to-beam ratio of the hull from three to one, increasing it to three and one-half to one and even four to one.[29] The greater length-to-beam ratio permitted a longer, slimmer bow with a galley-like beak. Improved stability was attained by lowering superstructures, particularly those in the forward part of the vessel, and relocating the guns from the upper decks to a lower level. These ships, which became known as Elizabethan galleons, were designed to fight with cannon, not with boarding parties.[30]

In 1587 Sir Francis Drake sailed into Cadiz with a few low-charge galleons and defeated about twelve oar-powered galleys led by Don Pedro de Acuña. Because of their oars, the galleys had more freedom of movement, but with their frail construction and their lack of broadside cannon they were no match for the heavy guns of the galleons, which had sufficient maneuverability to keep the galleys at a distance.[31] The Mediterranean type of oared war galleys were helpless against low-charge galleons.[32] Oar-powered galleys remained active warships in the Mediterranean, which was often windless, and

Figure 27. The low-charge galleon. Reducing the height of the forward superstructure improved performance to windward.

fought their last battle in 1717. They were also particularly effective along the Baltic coast where ragged rocks and islands placed the large square-rigged ships at a disadvantage; galleys were also active in the Russo-Swedish War of 1809.[33]

In 1588 Philip of Spain launched his Enterprise of England, which consisted of a total of 128 vessels, including four Portuguese galleys and four galleasses provided by the viceroy of Naples. To oppose the Spanish, the English had 102 ships.[34] The Spanish ships were larger and had the advantage in the number and size of guns by about a five to one ratio, but the range of the English cannon was greater. Also the English low-charge ships were about one-half knot faster and could sail one-half point (5.6 degrees) closer to the wind. The defeat of the Spanish Armada was not only due to the superior gunnery and maneuverability of the English ships, but also to the inability of the Spanish high-charge galleons to survive in the stormy waters of the British Isles. This nine-day battle is considered to be one of the world's most decisive because it marked Spain's decline as the world's greatest maritime power and the rise of England's control of the sea.[35]

THE FULL-RIGGED SHIP

In the early 1600s the sail plan of the galleon was gradually modified. The square sail located under the bowsprit (the spritsail) was too low to be an effective headsail, and an additional square sail (the spritsail topsail) was suspended from a short mast located at the tip of the bowsprit. The lateen topsail, on the mizzenmast and above the lateen steering sail, was replaced with a square sail. The bonaventure mast and its lateen sail was removed.[36] By 1650 the galleon had evolved into a three-masted ship equipped with only square sails, except for the lateen steering sail on the mizzen. The galleon is considered to be the first full-rigged ship, the first capital ship, and the first man-of-war. The three-masted low-charge design was eventually adopted by merchant vessels.

The
Square Rig

The sail arrangement of the full-rigged ship became known as the square-rig to differentiate it from the fore-and-aft sails introduced by the Dutch in the late fifteenth century. Ships equipped with predominantly square sails were referred to as square-riggers. In the seventeenth, eighteenth, and early nineteenth centuries a number of developments were implemented to improve the performance of sailing vessels.

STEERING

Steering is a major factor in a vessel's performance under sail. If the helmsman can observe the sails, he can often improve their performance by changing course slightly. This sort of maneuver requires a gentle positioning of the helm to prevent oversteering, which tends to result in a zigzag course. When the helm is put over, water flows against the rudder blade, turning the vessel and reducing its speed. Initially, sailors steered with paddles and later with oars. But the paddle or oar was not pivoted or hung; it was simply held by hand. The early Egyptians had two, three, and sometimes as many as five steering oars on each

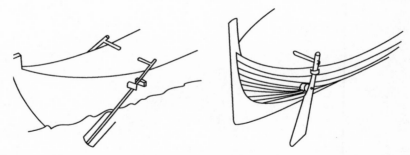

Figure 28. Side-mounted rudders. Two types were, *left,* the Mediterranean inclined rudder and, *right,* the Viking steerboard.

side. As the blade area of the steering oar increased, it was lashed to a cross beam, placed between two posts, or passed through a hole in a wooden block. Later, as early as the first century A.D., the Mediterranean sailors inclined their steering oar at about a 45-degree angle and attached it with a strap that allowed the blade to be rotated and function as a true rudder. They continued using this side-mounted rudder on each quarter.[1] The Viking steerboard was a more effective rudder because its rudder post was in a near vertical position; however, it became less effective when the vessel was heeled to port because the blade was no longer totally immersed, as can be seen in figure 28.

The stern-mounted hinged rudder was probably first introduced on the cog in about 1180.[2] It was a great improvement over the side rudder because it remained immersed at any angle of heel. Also, locating the rudder on a vertical post at the center of the stern meant that the hull no longer had to support a side rudder and could be narrowed toward the stern. This improved hull shape resulted in greater speed under sail.[3] The rudder was actuated by a horizontal lever called a tiller. However, the helmsman was positioned under the stern castle and could not observe the sail. This below deck area was called the steerage (fig. 29), and the name persisted to eventually describe a large below-deck area with bunks for passengers who could not afford a cabin.[4]

A later development, the whipstaff, consisted of a vertical lever attached to the tiller (fig. 30); this lever enabled the helmsman to be above deck where he could see the sails and adjust the ship's course for optimum performance. The whipstaff, however, could provide only a minimum rudder rotation to

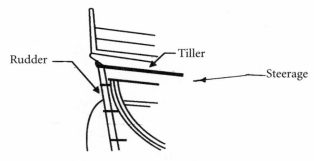

Figure 29. The centered stern-mounted rudder and tiller. The steerage is the below-deck space where the tiller was located.

each side, and mechanical advantage decreased when the helm was put over, so the assistance of a second helmsman was often required.[5] Today, a whipstaff steering system can be seen aboard the *Mayflower* replica at Plymouth, Massachusetts.

Near the end of the seventeenth century the wheel was introduced. This steering system was actually a windlass attached to the rudder by ropes, and it did not have to be on the same level as the top of the rudder (fig. 31). This arrangement provided greater force and range of rudder rotation, and it improved sailing performance by providing the helmsman with an excellent view of the sails.[6] An entire wheel-steering system is well displayed aboard the whaling bark *Charles W. Morgan* at the Mystic Seaport Museum in Mystic, Connecticut, and also aboard the brig *Pilgrim* in Dana Point, California.

COPPER SHEATHING

The portion of a ship's hull that extends below the water line attracts barnacles and other marine growth, reducing the life of a wood hull and severely decreasing speed under sail. In tropical waters, wooden hulls were particularly susceptible to the attack of the *teredo navalis* (shipworm), a large wood-boring worm. In 1761 copper sheathing was first applied to ships' bottoms to prevent sea growth and the attack of shipworms. This increased the life of the hull and resulted in a much smoother bottom and consequently more speed under sail. Earlier, sheathing with lead was attempted, but the lead accelerated corrosion of the iron rudder fittings.[7]

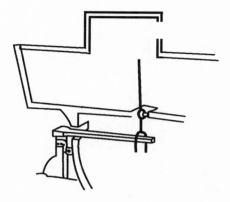

Figure 30. The whipstaff. Its placement such that the helmsman could see the sails.

ADDITIONAL SQUARE SAILS

The largest and principal sail on the foremast and on the mainmast of square-riggers was the lowest square sail; it was called the course. The course on the mainmast was the largest sail carried on the vessel and was called the mainsail (mains'l) as well as the main course. The sail immediately above was the topsail. Eventually, it was split into a lower and an upper topsail, as two smaller sails were easier to handle than the relatively large single topsail. The upper and lower topsail became the dominant sails as the courses were too big to handle effectively, and when the ship was entering or leaving port, the courses could be blanketed by structures on the shore. The higher, handier topsails provided better visibility and were large enough to reef when necessary. Warships eventually relied on their topsails for improved maneuverability in battle.[8]

Above the upper topsail was the topgallant sail. Toward the end of the eighteenth century masts were made taller: the royal sail was positioned above the topgallant and in the nineteenth, the skysail above the royal.[9]

FORE-AND-AFT SAILS

In the early 1700s, fore-and-aft sails developed by the Dutch (chap. 6) were added to the square-rigged ships. Jibs, triangular in shape, replaced the clumsy square sails located below and above the bowsprit. The jibs were located above the bowsprit and attached to jib-stays extending from the foremast to the bowsprit. Jibs functioned as propulsion sails and, because of their forward location, could also be adjusted to balance the helm and augment the function of the mizzen steering sail. Other triangular, jib-like sails were attached to the forestays—the forward centerline mast supports. These were propulsion sails and were called staysails.

Initially, the mizzenmast supported only the lateen steering sail. Later the mast was extended and an additional lateen was positioned above the steering sail. The upper lateen was then replaced with a square sail. (The square sails were suspended from horizontal spars, or yards, attached to the mast.) Another yard below the square sail was required to trim the square sail. This yard was called the *barren* yard because it did not support a square sail; that part of the lateen that extended forward of the mast would have interfered with the square sail.

This arrangement of sails lasted until about 1750.[10] At that time the Dutch modified the lateen sail, and the forward projection of the lateen was removed to create a gaff-rigged, fore-and-aft sail that hinged about the mast and was much easier to tack than the lateen. Within the next fifty years a boom was added to the foot of this sail to permit trimming it outboard when sailing off the wind. This fore-and-aft sail initially became known as the mizzen course.

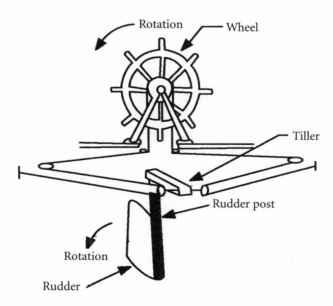

Figure 31. The wheel. Introduced in the early 1700s, this basic arrangement remains in use today.

Figure 32. The full-rigged ship with fore-and-aft jibs, staysails, and spanker. This rig of the early 1890s was still utilized by the early twentieth-century Cape Horners.

Next a square sail was suspended from the yard above the mizzen course, making it no longer a barren or empty yard. In turn, this square sail then became the mizzen course and the fore-and-aft steering sail became the spanker (fig. 32).[11]

HULL SHAPE

Frederik Hendrik Chapman (1721–1808) was the primary influence in optimizing the hull shape of sailing vessels of this era. He was born in Sweden and studied naval architecture in France, the Netherlands, and England, and in 1793 he was appointed chief testing constructor of the Swedish Navy. He built and used a test tank that drew ship models along the surface of the water using a clever system of drop weights. His test tank studies for speed made a long-lasting impact on naval architecture.[12]

FRIGATE DESIGN

The first true frigate prototype was a three-masted, square rigged, thirty-gun warship, built at the end of the seventeenth century. She had finer lines, less freeboard, and could sail faster than other contemporary vessels.[13] By the end of the eighteenth century virtually all of the square-rigged improvements were incorporated in the frigate. These nimble and speedy ships carried from twenty-four to thirty-eight guns and had sailing qualities superior to larger warships; they were used as fleet scouting vessels and in battle to repeat the admiral's signals to other ships of the line. Frigates also worked independently to search for privateers and to escort convoys.[14] The most famous frigate, the USS *Constitution*, "Old Ironsides," now over two hundred years old, remains a commissioned ship of the United States Navy and may be visited at the Charleston Navy Yard in Boston.

The merchant ship equivalent of the frigate was the East Indiaman. It was constructed and rigged in a similar manner to the frigate, but the East Indiaman did not carry royals and was the best full-rigged merchantman of the era. The British East India Company, in about 1675, established a shipyard in Bombay, India, for the construction of ships of Indian teak, considered to be the best ship timber to be found anywhere.[15] John Paul Jones's *Bonhomme Richard* was originally an East Indiaman but had been converted into a frigate prior to her famous action with the British frigate, HMS *Serapis,* on 23 September 1779.[16]

The Blackwall frigate was the name given to a series of sailing ships built between 1837 and 1869. They were not warships but got their name because many of them were built at Blackwall, on the Thames River, and the hull had the lines of a frigate and was considered frigate built, which made these ships faster than the typical East Indiaman. The Blackwall frigate *Seringapatum,* built in 1837, set a record of eighty-five days sailing from London to Bombay. These ships dominated the India trade until the opening of the Suez Canal in 1869.[17]

PACKETS

Traditionally, merchant sailing ships left port after they acquired a full cargo and with no forecast as to when they might arrive at their destination. But in the early 1800s (1818–1825) for the transatlantic trade, ships started to depart on a fixed date that was published in advance in newspapers. Because they carried packets of mail, these vessels came to be known as packets; and packet captains did their utmost to complete the voyage in a predictable period. Five to six weeks was the estimated voyage time from Liverpool to New York and three to four weeks from New York to Liverpool. The forces of nature—winds and currents—caused the difference in crossing times. The prevailing wind in the North Atlantic is from the northwest. A square-rigged ship could usually sail a direct course with little or no tacking when sailing east to Great Britain.

Also, it would be aided by the Gulf Stream, which flows northeastward in the North Atlantic. But sailing west from Liverpool to New York would require several long tacks, resulting in a longer, zigzagging route.

These packets were large ship-rigged merchantmen, and they were driven by their captains to meet the voyage time commitment. The main emphasis was passenger comfort. Eventually packets provided individual staterooms that were eight feet square and finished in polished matched-grain wood, and included stands, bureaus, bookshelves, and a bed closed in by damask curtains. By 1840 these ships were 166 feet long and 350 tons. Unlike most merchantmen, the packets remained in service for only about six years and were then replaced with ships that offered more elegance.[18]

6

The
Fore-and-Aft
Rig

The Dutch had a unique problem. They had many inland waterways, but they also sailed the North Sea. The Viking square sail did not permit sailing close enough to the wind to sail a desired course in inland waterways, and the lateen with its enormous yard was not suitable for the severe winds and heavy seas of the North Sea.[1]

THE DUTCH DEVELOPMENT

It is generally believed that in the fifteenth century,[2] the Dutch deleted that part of the lateen sail that extended forward of the mast and supported the sail with a spar (sprit) that extended from the base of the mast to the peak of the sail (fig. 33). This modification of the lateen became known as a fore-and-aft spritsail and eliminated the need for repositioning the yard when the vessel was tacking since both the sail and sprit hinged on the mast. Historians have determined that the spritsail was in use from the north Aegean to Rome as early as the second century B.C. In *Ships and Seamanship in the Ancient World,* Lionel Casson presents photographs of second- and first-century B.C.

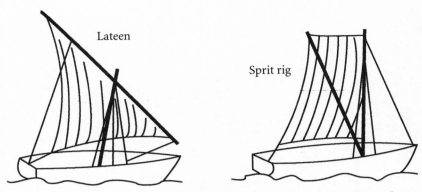

Figure 33. *Left:* the original lateen sail. *Right:* the fore-and-aft spritsail—the Dutch modification of the lateen sail. The spritsail had better windward performance than the lateen and was easier to tack.

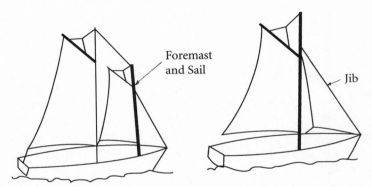

Figure 34. *Right to left:* the jib replaces the foremast and sail. The jib vastly improved windward performance.

masonry reliefs showing a rectangular sail with the luff attached to the mast and a diagonal sprit supporting the upper after corner,[3] but the Dutch sail was not rectangular. It seems feasible that the Dutch development could have been independent of the earlier spritsail.

In about 1523, the Dutch next replaced the cumbersome sprit with a smaller spar called a gaff. This was initially called the half-sprit rig. In the early seventeenth century, another spar called a boom was attached to the foot of the sail to permit trimming the sail outboard for sailing off the wind.[4] After their modification of the lateen, the Dutch installed two fore-and-aft

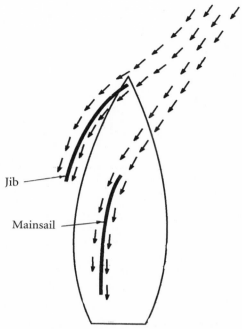

Figure 35. The mainsail *lifts* the jib. Lift means that the wind striking the sail is from further aft.

sails on two masts of their larger vessels. Around 1600, however, they determined that the forward mast and sail could be replaced with a single triangular sail suspended from the forward support (stay) of the remaining mast.[5] This modification is shown in figure 34. This sail, located ahead of the remaining mast, turned out to be exceptionally effective in sailing to windward and proved to be a major breakthrough for sailing against the wind.

The long sloping leading edge of the sail provided a long luff (ideal for sailing to windward) that remained rigid because it was attached to the forestay (the rope supporting the mast). Moreover, there was no spar to disturb the airflow over the forward part of the sail. In addition, a unique interaction occurs between the sail attached to the mast (the aftersail) and the sail ahead of the mast (the headsail). The aftersail actually changes the direction of the wind stream that strikes the headsail (fig. 35), so that the wind approaches from further aft, and the aftersail *lifts* the headsail (when the wind shifts ahead, the vessel is said to be *headed;* when the wind shifts aft, the vessel is *lifted*).[6]

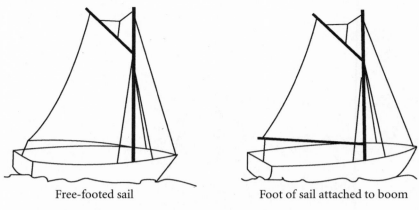

Free-footed sail   Foot of sail attached to boom

Figure 36. The fore-and-aft gaff sail: free footed, and attached to a boom, which provides a greater effective sail area when the wind is from the stern.

Vessels of all sizes began using this triangular sail, including square-rigged ships. When positioned over the bowsprit, these sails were called jibs, and when they were attached to the stays that supported the mast, they were known as staysails. On today's recreational sailboats, however, the headsail attached to the forestay is called a jib.

THE SPRIT RIG

The spritsail with the jib headsail became known as the sprit rig and was the first practical sail arrangement for use both at sea and along inland waters.[7] This rig permitted sailing to about 52 degrees of the true wind, better than the 56.25 degrees of the lateen; tacking was simplified, and a smaller crew was required, as was shown in figure 33. The first seagoing vessel built in the American colonies (1640) was the sprit-rigged *Virginia*.

GAFF RIG

The fore-and-aft gaff sail with jib became known as a gaff-rigged fore-and-aft rig (fig. 36). It permits sailing to about 50 degrees of the true wind and is currently used on some recreational sailboats.

Figure 37. The Bermuda fore-and-aft rig. Elimination of the gaff provides a better sail shape at the top of the sail when sailing to windward and improves windward performance. But a taller mast is required to obtain the same sail area as with the gaff sail.

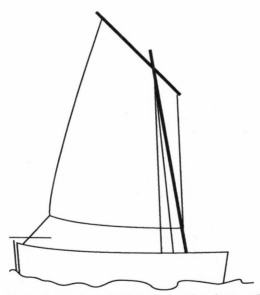

Figure 38. The dipping lug fore-and-aft rig. This rig provides a better sail shape because the lug is always on the leeward side.

Figure 39. The standing lug fore-and-aft rig. This rig is easier to tack because the lug remains on the same side of the mast.

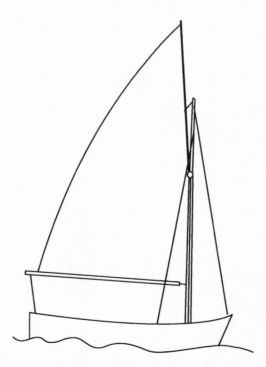

Figure 40. The gunter fore-and-aft rig. The almost vertical gaff makes the gunter almost comparable to the Bermuda rig.

THE BERMUDA RIG

Later, the gaff was deleted, and this arrangement was called a Bermuda or Bermudan rig (fig. 37) because it was first used in the West Indies in the early 1800s.[8] This rig is also known as the Marconi rig and the sail as a leg-o'-mutton sail.[9] Most of today's recreational sailboats use the Bermuda rig and can sail within 45 degrees of the true wind.

The Bermuda rig has a particularly important advantage for today's racing sailboats. Because the sail is almost a true triangular shape, the sail can be flattened by tensioning the lower edge (the foot) and slightly bending (bowing) the mast. Sails flattened in this manner allow today's Bermuda-rigged racing yachts to sail within 39 degrees of the true wind, but under favorable wind and sea condition, high-performance racing yachts can sail to within less than 39 degrees.[10] America's Cup twelve-meter racing yachts, for example, have actually sailed to within 32 degrees of the wind, closer than any other vessel.[11]

LUGGER RIG

This rig is similar to the fore-and-aft gaff rig except that the gaff (called the lug) extends forward of the mast and normally there is no boom attached to the foot of the sail. The two common lugger rigs are the dipping lug (fig. 38) and the standing lug (fig. 39). A third type of lugger rig—the balanced lug—is actually a standing lug with a boom at the foot of the sail. A variation of the standing lug is known as the gunter rig (fig. 40), in which the gaff is almost vertical making the sail similar in effect to the Bermuda rig.[12]

On the dipping-lug version of this rig, the lug and sail are always on the leeward side of the mast. This provides the best sail shape but makes tacking difficult. When the vessel is tacking, the halyard must be loosened to lower the lug, and when the vessel is head to the wind, the lug and sail are shifted to the new leeward side. The halyard is then tightened. This procedure, called dipping the lug, is complicated, and to minimize the complexity of this procedure, a relatively small portion of the lug and sail extend forward of the mast.

In the standing lug arrangement about one-third of the lug and sail are forward of the mast. Tacking is no problem as the lug and sail always remain on the same side of the mast. On one tack, the lug and sail are on the leeward side of the mast; and on the opposite tack, they are on the windward side. Sailing vessels with lugsails became known as luggers.

Luggers were popular in the seventeenth, eighteenth, and nineteenth centuries in Europe as small fishing and coastal craft because they were fast and

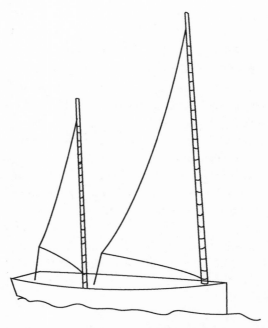

Figure 41. The leg-o'-mutton sprit fore-and-aft rig. This is the simplest fore-and-aft rig because the sail is permanently attached to the mast.

could sail well to windward. The balanced lug was popular in the Adriatic.[13] The French chasse-marée luggers (a chasse-marée was a coastal vessel that worked the tide) were used as smugglers and privateers because of their exceptional performance to windward.[14] Although a 1584 painting by a Dutch artist shows a lugsail, there is evidence that this sail preceded the Dutch conversion of the lateen into fore-and-aft sails.

Though square sails were commonly used on the west coast of India, a wall painting from the sixth century A.D. in one of India's famous Ajanta caves shows a vessel with lugsails.[15] The sail of the Chinese junk can be classified as a balanced lugsail.

THE LEG-O'-MUTTON SPRIT RIG

This rig, a fore-and-aft sail arrangement in its simplest form, consisted of a triangular leg-o'-mutton sail attached directly to an unstayed mast (fig. 41). Early American small sailing craft were equipped with this sail because of its simplicity. It continued to be used on whale boats. After the whalers chased the whale under oars, they made the return trip under a spritsail, which was also used on New England fishing dories. The origin of the leg-o'-mutton sprit rig probably preceded the Dutch modification of the lateen because some evidence suggests that it was used much earlier on small craft in the Mediterranean.[16]

THE LATEEN RIG

The aforementioned rigs permit trimming the sail close to the vessel's fore-and-aft centerline. Hence they are categorized as fore-and-aft rigs. The lateen (fig. 10) cannot be trimmed completely to a vessel's centerline because the lower, forward end of the diagonal yard is always on the windward side of the vessel; however, the lateen rig is classified as the world's first fore-and-aft sail.[17]

Two
Classic Sailing
Rigs

Through the centuries there evolved two basic types of sails: the square sail used on ships commonly called square riggers, and the fore-and-aft sails. Each type has its advantages and disadvantages and each has been supplemented with sails from the other category.

THE SQUARE RIG

The square-rigged ship is faster than a comparable fore-and-aft rigged vessel when the apparent wind is from aft to slightly forward of the beam. Wide yardarms and the ability to position one square sail above another results in a significantly larger total sail area than can be obtained with fore-and-aft sails, and sail area is the dominant factor when sailing off the wind.

The square-rigged ship could at best sail only to about 67.5 degrees of the true wind,[1] but this was not a significant disadvantage because of the circular wind patterns of the Atlantic and Pacific (fig. 42). Ocean-voyaging ships would usually sail westward near the equator to take advantage of the trade winds blowing from east to west, then northward, aided by the warm Japanese current in the Pacific and the Gulf Stream in the Atlantic, and they would

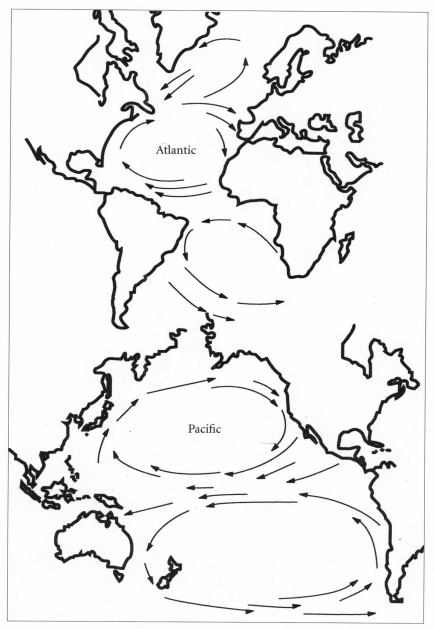

Figure 42. Circular wind patterns in the Atlantic and the Pacific Oceans.

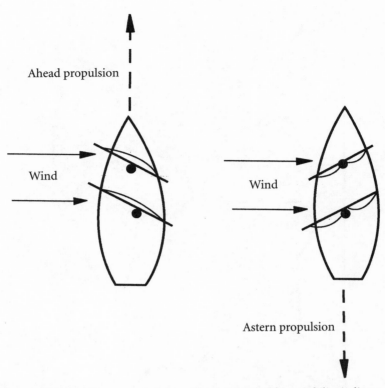

Ahead propulsion

Wind

Wind

Astern propulsion

Figure 43. Ahead and astern propulsion with square sails. This capability indicates a definite advantage of the square rig over the fore-and-aft rig.

return easterly when in high latitudes to take advantage of the prevailing northwesterly winds. For this reason, ships making ocean passages were usually full-rigged ships.

The trade-wind route in the Pacific was established by the Spanish in about 1570. They sailed their galleons from Acapulco, Mexico, to Manila, in the Philippines, taking advantage of the trade winds blowing from the east. A reverse route was not feasible as these early square-riggers were ill-suited for sailing against the wind. Instead, the galleons' return voyage consisted of riding the warm Japanese current northward and then southeasterly along the west coast of North America. This allowed them to claim possession of California for Spain.

The slave trade in the Atlantic was known as the triangular trade (also known as the blackbird trade).[2] From New England, the slave ships carried beads, tin pans, and calico, following the Gulf Stream across the Atlantic and then south to the west coast of Africa, where the cargo was sold or bartered for slaves. The slave ships then sailed west along the trade wind belt to the West Indies where the slaves were sold or bartered for rum. The ships then rode the Gulf Stream northward back to New England.

Another advantage of square sails over fore-and-aft sails was that, except when vessels were sailing in a general downwind direction, the square sails could be repositioned (back winded) to provide astern propulsion and allow the square-rigger to sail backwards (fig. 43).[3] In the early 1800s New England ship owners sent ships around the Horn to trade with settlements along the California coast. The preferred vessel for this employment was a small, shallow-draft, square-rigged vessel. The California waters at that time were completely uncharted and when ships were approaching a desired anchorage, there was always a danger of going aground. When vessels encountered a sudden shoaling, the square sails could be immediately backed to provide astern propulsion and allow the square-rigger to sail backwards out of the danger area.[4]

This period of California history is well documented in Richard Henry Dana's *Two Years Before the Mast*. Dana (1815–1882) was a Harvard student who interrupted his studies to serve as a seaman *before the mast* (in the days of sail, the officers quarters were located in the after part of the vessel and seamen were berthed in the forecastle, located ahead of the foremast). He served most of his two years aboard the brig *Pilgrim*, which sailed around Cape Horn and traded for hides along the California coast. At today's Dana Point, hides were purchased from the San Juan Capistrano Mission, about two miles inland. Upon his return to Boston, about two years later, Dana wrote his memorable book describing the hardships experienced by American seamen at that time and was instrumental in improving working conditions for all merchant seamen.[5]

The greatest disadvantage of the full-rigged ship was the difficulty of sail handling. The square sails were suspended from yards. To take the sail in and tie it down or to release it, the crew had to stand on toe ropes attached to the yards. This was a dangerous and time-consuming process, particularly in rough or freezing weather. For this reason the full-rigged ship required a large crew.

Although square-rigged vessels were eventually equipped with some fore-and-aft sails, they were classified as square-riggers if their main driving sails were suspended from yards, regardless of the number of additional fore-and-aft sails. The basic square-rigged vessels were the ship, bark, brig, and the

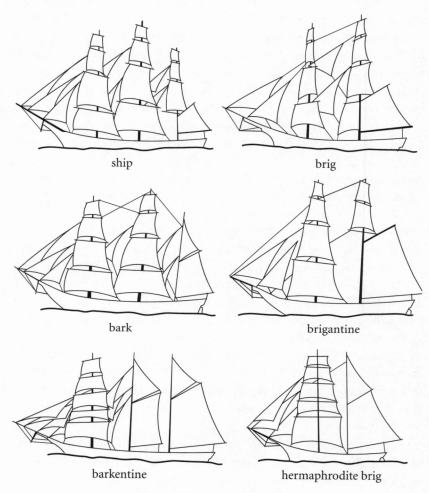

ship   brig

bark   brigantine

barkentine   hermaphrodite brig

Figure 44. Square-rigged vessels.

The brig *Pilgrim* off Dana Point, California. The Ocean Institute's brig *Pilgrim* provides a national award-winning living history program to over sixteen thousand students a year. The *Pilgrim* also hosts a variety of maritime dramatic and musical theatrical performances during the summer months in its home port of Dana Point.
Bob Grieser

hermaphrodite brig. The barkentine and the brigantine are also classified as square-rigged vessels, although in some cases they carry as many—or more—fore-and-aft sails as they do square sails (fig. 44).[6] The ship, bark, and barkentine were mostly three-masted, but some were built with four and even five masts. The brig, hermaphrodite brig, and the brigantine were always two-masted.

A model of the ship *Euterpe* at the Maritime Museum of San Diego, California.
Leo Block

Another model of the same ship showing her re-rigged as a bark and renamed the *Star of India,* also at the Maritime Museum of San Diego.
Leo Block

The *snow* was a brig with the steering sail attached to a small mast located immediately aft of the mainmast.[7] Some snows had an additional small mast immediately aft of the foremast to support a gaff-rigged fore-and-aft sail called the *spencer*.[8] With all square sails furled and sailing only with the spencer, spanker, jibs, and stay sails, the vessel would sail much closer to the wind than with square sails. The snow rig with spencer can now be seen aboard the *Pilgrim* (a replica of Dana's *Pilgrim*) at Dana Point, California.

The intent of intermingling masts with square sails and masts with fore-and-aft sails was to obtain an optimum balance of pointing ability and speed off the wind that would best suit the employment of the vessel. Also, crew size was a factor. San Diego's *Star of India* was initially a full-rigged ship, the *Euterpe,* but was converted into a bark when purchased by the Alaska Packers Association, since a bark would better meet their need for operations in Alaska waters. The ship *Euterpe,* named for the ancient Greek muse of music, was launched at Ramsey, Isle of Man, in 1863. Her initial voyages were to India, and later she transported settlers to New Zealand, carrying 416 tightly packed passengers per trip. She survived a mutiny and later a cyclone by having her topmasts cut away. It was in 1901 that she was purchased by the Alaska Packers Association, rerigged as a bark, and her name changed to the *Star of India*. In 1926 she was purchased by an ambitious group of San Diegans, who hoped to restore the vessel. From 1926 through the years of the Depression and World War II, little or no improvements were made on the vessel. The owners just managed to keep her afloat and pay the docking fees. But after the war, improvements began to be made. In 1976 she sailed for the first time in fifty years and now sails at sea on numerous special occasions. The *Star of India,* maintained by the San Diego Maritime Museum, is the oldest active sailing vessel in the world.[9]

THE FORE-AND-AFT RIG

Although slower off the wind than square-rigged ships (because of less sail area), the fore-and-aft vessels had the advantage of sailing much closer to the wind, and for this reason they were commonly used as coastal and inland waterway vessels. Tacking was a relatively simple maneuver because the sails pivoted about their mast or support stay (except for the spinnaker), and a smaller crew was required because from deck level the sails could be raised, lowered, and reefed.

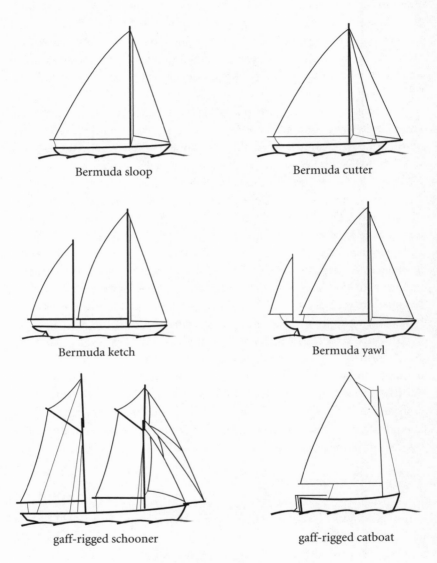

Bermuda sloop

Bermuda cutter

Bermuda ketch

Bermuda yawl

gaff-rigged schooner

gaff-rigged catboat

Figure 45. Fore-and-aft-rigged vessels.

If the luff of the sail abuts a mast or is attached to a stay, the rig is classified as fore-and-aft: the sloop, cutter, catboat, ketch, yawl, and schooner are fore-and-aft-rigged vessels (fig. 45). To improve their downwind performance, the sloop, cutter, and schooner were frequently equipped with square sails but were still classified as fore-and-aft-rigged vessels. The sloop, cutter, and catboat are always single masted. The sloop carries a single jib and the cutter has two head-sails (jib and staysail). Most of today's recreational sailboats are sloops, but the cutter rig is popular for larger cruising boats because two headsails are easier to handle than one large jib on a sloop of comparable size. The single mast of the catboat is stepped in the bow and supports a Bermuda or gaff-rig sail. It originated in Cape Cod in the nineteenth century to use for fishing in shallow water and was later adapted for coastal cruising and racing.[10] Its major feature is ease of handling as there is only one sail, but the absence of a jib reduces its windward performance.

The tallest mast is the forward mast on the ketch. In the seventeenth and eighteenth centuries the ketch was equipped with square sails. Today's ketch evolved from the bomb ketch, a formerly three-masted ship with the foremast removed to provide space for the mortar from which the bomb was fired.[11] But after about 1801 the British bomb vessel was no longer a ketch. It was a three-masted, ship-rigged vessel with two mortars. One was located between the foremast and mainmast, and the other between the mainmast and mizzen. These ships were constructed to withstand the tremendous recoil of the mortars, and the ship rig gave them improved sailing qualities.[12] After use of the bomb vessel died out in the nineteenth century, sailors installed fore-and-aft sails on the two-masted vessels to improve upwind performance. They were then used as coastal vessels and are now popular among cruising yachtsmen because of the ease of handling several smaller sails compared to the fewer but larger sails on a same size sloop or cutter.

The yawl is similar to a ketch except the after (mizzen) mast is much smaller and is positioned aft of the rudderpost, whereas the mizzenmast on a ketch is stepped forward of the rudderpost.

In 1927 an oversize jib that overlapped the mainsail was introduced in a regatta in Genoa, Italy, by the Swedish yachtsman Sven Salen[13] and is now known as a genoa jib (fig. 46). It improved the performance of the fore-and-aft rig by increasing the velocity of the airflow on the leeward (downwind) side of the mainsail and is now used routinely on racing yachts and some cruising yachts except under strong wind conditions. New materials for sails,

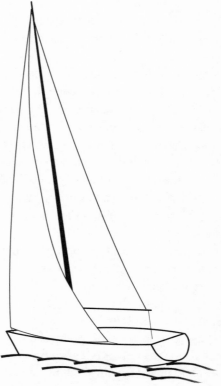

Figure 46. The genoa overlapping jib. Commonly used on today's racing yachts.

spars, rigging, and hull construction have improved the performance of today's fore-and-aft racing and cruising sailing vessels; but the fundamental principal of operation is the same as developed by the Dutch in the fifteenth and sixteenth centuries.

Two additional vessels, the xebec and the polacre, can probably best be described as having conversion rigs. Both were used only from the sixteenth to the nineteenth centuries in the Mediterranean and were quite similar. They were two-masted or three-masted vessels with lateen sails on all masts; this gave them excellent windward performance. But when the wind was from abaft the beam, one or more of the lateen sails were replaced with square sails. This complex conversion required a large crew, but because of the excellent upwind and off the wind performance, these rigs were favored in the

Mediterranean by corsairs during the 1700s and 1800s. The vessels carried a crew of three hundred to four hundred and could attain a greater speed at any point of sail than their victims.[14]

NOMENCLATURE

Today, the word *ship* pertains to a seagoing vessel large enough to make ocean voyages safely and with a reasonable degree of comfort; but in the days of sail, ship was used to describe a vessel with a ship rig. A schooner was not called a ship, nor was a brig, nor were other vessels with two masts. The word *ship* was reserved for a sailing vessel with three or more masts and with square sails on each mast. There were, however, exceptions.

Capt. James Cook's *Endeavour* was classified as a bark although she was equipped with square sails on all three masts. In the rigorous definition of *ship,* the sailing vessel must have three or more masts, and each mast must consist of three sections (lower mast, topmast, and topgallant mast) and include a square sail in each section. The *Endeavour*'s mizzen consisted only of two sections and therefore she could not be classified as a ship. She was also not a true bark as she was equipped with a square sail on the mizzen in addition to a fore-and-aft steering sail. At that time, the term *bark* was also a general designation for a small shiplike vessel; thus, the bark *Endeavour*.[15]

Also, the word *ship* was not normally applied to warships, even though most were ship rigged (brigs and cutters were not). Instead, warships were categorized by the positioning of the guns.

Sloop of war

A warship with all guns located on the spar (upper) deck was called a sloop of war (or sloop o' war) although she was ship rigged (three masts with square sails on each mast). The French called such warships corvettes. John Paul Jones's famous *Ranger* was a sloop o'war.

Frigate

A larger vessel with more guns was the frigate, also ship rigged but with guns located on two levels: on the spar deck and on the gun (lower) deck. The USS *Constitution* presently in the Boston Navy Yard is a large frigate.

Ship of the line

A ship of the line was the largest warship, also ship rigged and with guns on three levels: on the spar deck and on two (lower) gun decks. Adm. Horatio Nelson's flagship, the HMS *Victory*, at the Battle of Trafalgar was a ship of the line.

Another anomaly of nomenclature was the U.S. Revenue Cutter Service's practice of designating their larger vessels as cutters when most were rigged as topsail schooners. The *Californian*, a topsail schooner homeported in Long Beach, California, is a replica of a nineteenth-century so-called cutter. The Revenue Cutter Service was founded in 1790 with ten vessels to stamp out piracy and smuggling and was the nation's only naval force until 1798, when the United States Navy was reestablished (primarily to keep Barbary pirates from demanding tribute from American ships and taking U.S. seamen hostage, for whom they demanded a ransom). In 1915 the Revenue Cutter Service was combined with the Life Saving Service to form the United States Coast Guard; their largest power vessels are still classified as cutters.

The term *spritsail* could also cause confusion because it was used to describe three vastly different sails. Originally it was the name of the square sail located under the bowsprit; spritsail topsail was the square sail flown from the short mast at the tip of the bowsprit.[16] Later, the spritsail was the four-sided fore-and-aft sail of the sprit rig;[17] and finally, it was the triangular, leg-o'-mutton sail attached directly to the unstayed mast on early American small sailing craft.[18]

THE FIGUREHEAD AND OTHER CUSTOMS OF SAILING

In the days of sail the figurehead was a decorative emblem, but earlier, it was both a religious symbol and a figurative representation that the ship was a living thing. The ancient Egyptians painted eyes on the bow so the ship could see where it was going. The Phoenicians used a horse's head to symbolize vision and swiftness, and the Greeks, a boar's head for ferociousness. Roman ships often displayed a carving of a centurion to imply fighting ability. The Vikings preferred a serpent's head.

The popularity of the figurehead declined after the development of the carrack and the galleon. On these vessels the forecastles were built above and beyond the ship's stem, leaving no suitable location for a figurehead. By about 1700 the structure extending over the bow was eliminated, and the space below the bowsprit and adjacent to the stem provided an ideal location for a figurehead. English warships preferred a lion or a tiger. The Dutch and Spanish also preferred the lion, and the French ships carried figureheads of Neptune or Jupiter.

Sailors during the Age of Sail were extremely superstitious. From ancient days when a ship was launched or about to embark on a long voyage, it was a custom to offer a libation to the gods of the sea by pouring wine upon the deck. Today, a bottle of wine is broken across the bow of a ship when she is launched. Friday was an unlucky day to start a voyage. Women on board were also considered to be bad luck. Even as late as the nineteenth century, a fisherman in the Firth of Forth would refuse to go to sea if a barefooted woman crossed his path while he was on the way to his boat. Yet many seamen believed that gales and high winds would subside if a naked woman appeared before them. It was this superstition that by the 1800s led to a figurehead of a comely lass showing one or both naked breasts so that her influence would calm the severest wind and tame a stormy sea.[19]

INTO THE TWENTIETH CENTURY

The introduction of steam propulsion (1800) did not immediately terminate the Age of Sail. Clipper ships were developed in the mid-1800s and proved to be much faster than steamers of that era. The Chilean nitrate trade required sailing vessels to sail around Cape Horn; this route was not feasible for steamships due to the lack of coaling stations. The Cape Horners built for this Chilean nitrate trade were built of steel. Steel plates could be one-fifth thinner than iron and still have the same strength, resulting in a weight reduction of 15 percent. Tubular steel masts permitted weight reduction aloft; wire rope was used for the standing rigging, and flexible wire rope was used for the running rigging. The use of winches instead of tackle permitted a reduction in the size of the crew. Most of these ships were rigged as three- or four-masted barks and had a much larger cargo capacity than the clippers but were only a few knots slower.[20] These powerful steel-hulled ships were built mostly in Britain, Germany, and Finland as late as the early 1900s. The last surviving steel-hulled sailing ship is the *Balclutha;* she was built in 1886 in Glasgow and fully restored to her original state in 1954 by the San Francisco Maritime Museum Association.[21] (The *Balclutha* is open to visitors.)

The largest sailing ship built was the *Prussen*, a five-masted fully rigged ship of 11,150 tons, built in Germany in 1902 and wrecked in 1910. After a collision with a steamer in the English Channel, the *Prussen* attempted to sail into Dover Harbor. But a gale blew up and despite the assistance of three tugs, the injured ship drifted along the Dover mole and piled herself onto the rocks below Dover's famous White Cliffs.[22] The *Prussen* was 433 feet long and 54 feet wide; she carried fifteen to eighteen fore-and-aft sails with a total sail area of 60,000 square feet and required a crew of forty-seven.[23]

Because these ships were fully paid for and crew labor was cheap, use of some of these square-riggers extended into the depression years of the 1930s. Square-rigged ships carried grain from Australia to England and Europe until World War II.[24] In fact, one sailing vessel saw service as a cargo carrier during World War II. The *Kenilworth* was a four-masted bark built in 1887. She was burned in 1889 and rebuilt because her iron hull was undamaged. Later, the *Kenilworth* was purchased by the Alaska Packers Association, and her name was changed to the *Star of Scotland.* In 1930 she served as a fishing barge anchored off the Southern California coast at Santa Monica. In 1938 and 1939 she became the gambling ship *Rex* and was anchored three and a half miles off shore. After the start of World War II, when ships of all types were in great demand, she was rerigged as a schooner and was carrying a cargo of lumber when she was sunk off the coast of Africa by a German submarine in 1942.[25]

A model of the *Prussen,* the largest sailing ship ever built, on display at the San Francisco Historic Park, San Francisco, California.
Leo Block

Points

of

Sail

A point of sail is the general orientation of a vessel under sail relative to the true wind. The points of sail for the square rig and the fore-and-aft rig are shown in figures 47 and 48. A vessel sailing close hauled, that is, sailing as close as it can to the direction from which the wind is blowing, is said to be sailing on the wind, and in the days of sail this point of sail was known as *full and by.* When the wind is from slightly further aft, the vessel is on a *close reach* and is sailing free or off the wind. When the wind is from the general direction of the beam, the vessel is on a *reach* or *beam reach* and may be referred to as reaching across the wind or sailing across the wind. When the wind is blowing from approximately 45 degrees from the stern, the vessel is on a *broad reach* and is running free—or running with the wind. Sailing directly down wind is a *run*—or running before the wind.[1] It is important to note that these points of sail are relative to the true wind not the apparent wind.

Sailing close hauled is typically the slowest point of sail. A change in course that allows the wind to approach the beam usually results in the vessel sailing faster until the maximum speed is attained with the wind at or near the

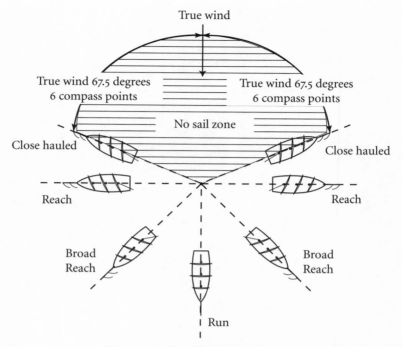

Figure 47. Points of sail on a square rig.

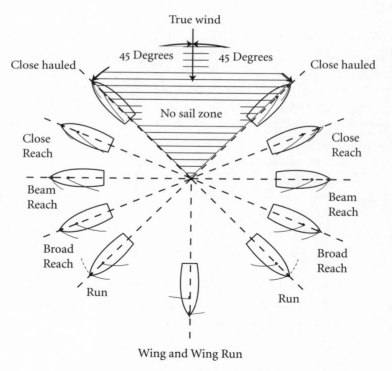

Figure 48. Points of sail on a fore-and-aft rig.

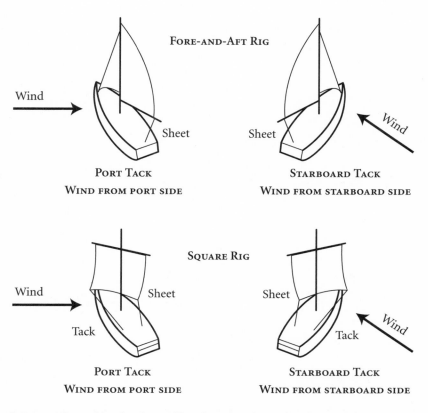

FORE-AND-AFT RIG

Wind

Sheet

Sheet

Wind

PORT TACK
WIND FROM PORT SIDE

STARBOARD TACK
WIND FROM STARBOARD SIDE

SQUARE RIG

Wind

Sheet

Sheet

Wind

Tack

Tack

PORT TACK
WIND FROM PORT SIDE

STARBOARD TACK
WIND FROM STARBOARD SIDE

Figure 49. The starboard tack vessel has the right-of-way over the port-tack vessel unless she is the overtaking vessel.

beam. The speed drops off when the wind is on the quarter; and when the wind is brought to nearly dead astern, there is a further reduction in speed, depending on how some sails block the wind from reaching other sails (creating a wind shadow or blanketing of sails).

When sailing with the wind abeam, from close reaching to broad reaching, every sail develops full power and is little affected by wind eddies. This orientation provides the maximum speed in sailing. The peculiarity of the rig can affect the point of sail for maximum speed. Square-rigged vessels usually attain maximum speed when sailing on a broad reach, as long as all sails can be filled without interfering with the wind to another sail. Fore-and-aft vessels usually sail faster on a reach or even a close reach.[2]

Normally, a square-rigged vessel would not sail directly downwind; the

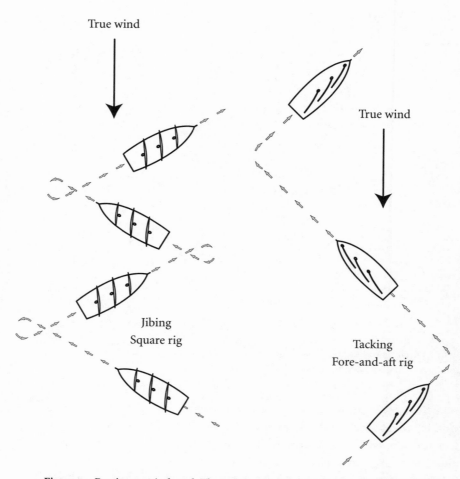

True wind

True wind

Jibing
Square rig

Tacking
Fore-and-aft rig

Figure 50. Beating to windward. The square-rigged vessel cannot always tack, but she can always jibe.

aftermost sails would block the wind from the other sails (the forward sails would be in the wind shadow of the after sails). Instead, she would jibe downwind to insure that the wind strikes all the sails. The increase in speed attained by exposing all the square sails to the wind would result in a faster voyage, although the distance traveled would be greater.[3]

PORT TACK AND STARBOARD TACK

When it is sailing on any point of sail (except directly downwind on the square-rig), a vessel is said to be sailing on the *starboard tack* if the wind is from starboard and on the *port tack* when the wind is from the port side (fig. 49). The nautical rules of the road specify that when two sailing vessels are on a collision course, the vessel sailing on the starboard tack has the right of way (unless she is the overtaking vessel), and the port-tack vessel must change course or speed to keep clear. If both vessels are sailing on the same tack, the leeward (downwind) vessel has the right of way.

BEAT TO WINDWARD

A sailing vessel cannot sail directly into the wind, the "no sail zone" in figures 47 and 48. To proceed in this direction, the vessel must sail a zigzag route by first sailing close hauled on one tack (for example, the starboard tack) and then sail close hauled on the opposite tack (for example, the port tack), and later turning to sail again on the original tack. Continuing this shifting from one tack to the other, a sailing vessel can gradually proceed toward the direction from which the wind is blowing. Sailing this zigzag path to windward is known as a *beat to windward* (fig. 50). In making the turn from one tack to the opposite tack, a vessel can either tack (turn so that the bow of the vessel passes through the direction of the true wind) or jibe (turn so that the stern passes through the direction of the true wind). Jibing is also known as *wear ship*. When beating to windward, tacking is the preferred maneuver; jibing is less desirable because distance is lost by turning away from the destination.

Because of the arrangement of the sails and rigging, the fore-and-aft rig is best suited for tacking and the square rig for jibing. Rigging is any rope, wire, or chain used to support spars, hoist yards and sails, or trim sails. A spar is any rigid support for a sail such as a mast boom, yard (yardarm), gaff, or

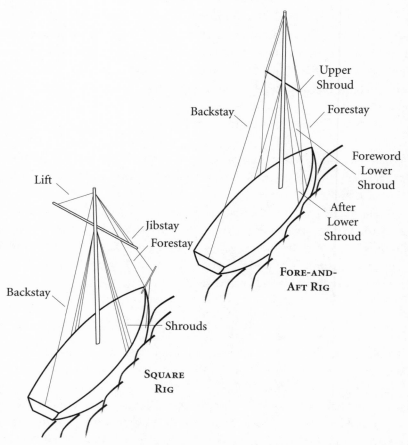

Figure 51. Elements of standing rigging.

bowsprit. Standing rigging is semipermanent rigging used to support masts, yards, and the bowsprit (fig. 51); running rigging is movable and is used to hoist yards, gaffs, sails, and trim sails (fig. 52).

To tack with the square sail, the vessel must have sufficient momentum, prior to the turn, to overcome the tendency for the wind to drive the vessel backward at the start of the turn. Before the turn, the jib sheets are let go (to allow the bow to turn into the wind), and the spanker is hauled to windward (to force the stern downwind). After the vessel is head to wind, the back-winded foresails force the bow down to the new course. The sails are then hauled so that the wind strikes their after side (fig. 53). Tacking is not feasi-

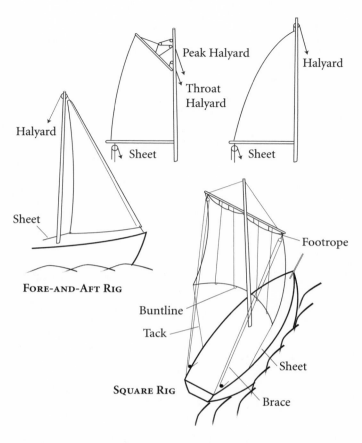

Peak Halyard

Halyard

Throat
Halyard

Halyard

Sheet

Sheet

Halyard

Footrope

Sheet

FORE-AND-AFT RIG

Buntline

Tack

Sheet

SQUARE RIG

Brace

Figure 52. Elements of running rigging.

ble in extreme light wind (insufficient momentum), and an exceptionally strong wind may damage sails, rigging, and spars. Tacking the fore-and-aft rig is a much simpler maneuver because all sails hinge about a mast or a stay. When the vessel turns into the wind, the sails flap and hinge about their vertical support. After the turn, the sails again draw with the wind impinging on their opposite side (fig. 54).

When square rigged vessels cannot tack, they must resort to jibing, a slow but relatively simple maneuver (fig. 55). There are two distinct types of jibes for the fore-and-aft rig: the controlled jibe and the accidental (or inadvertent) jibe—which can be extremely dangerous. For the fore-and-aft-controlled

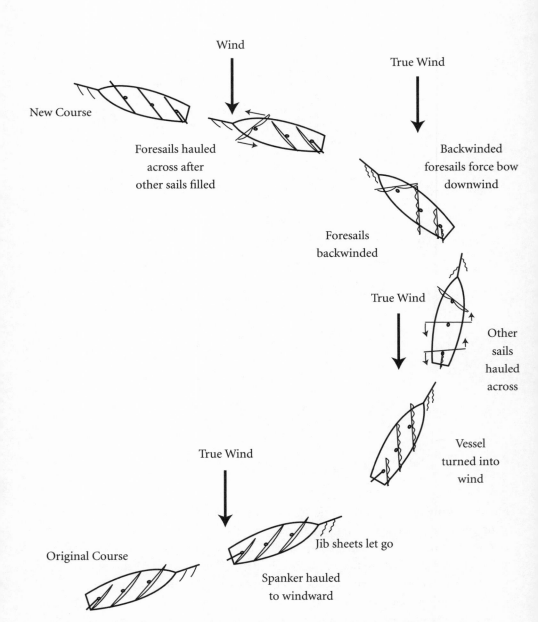

Figure 53. Tacking the square rig. A very light wind may not provide sufficient momentum to tack. An exceptionally strong wind may damage sails and rigging.

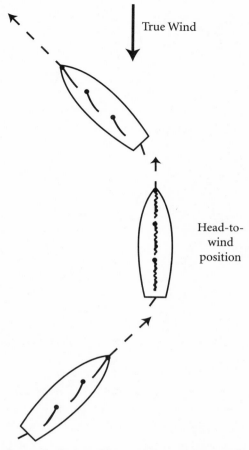

True Wind

Head-to-wind position

Figure 54. Tacking the fore-and-aft rig. Before tacking, the vessel must have sufficient momentum to pass through the head-to-wind position.

jibe, the sheet attached to the boom must be gradually tightened while the vessel is turning in the downwind direction. The sheet must be at maximum tightness when the boom is on the vessel centerline, and the wind starts to impinge on the opposite side of the sail. Then, as the turn continues, the sheet is gradually eased until the sail and boom are in the desired position (fig. 56).

Sailing directly downwind in a fore-and-aft-rigged vessel during rough weather can cause an accidental jibe when a following or quartering sea suddenly turns the vessel so that the wind strikes the opposite side of the sail. The

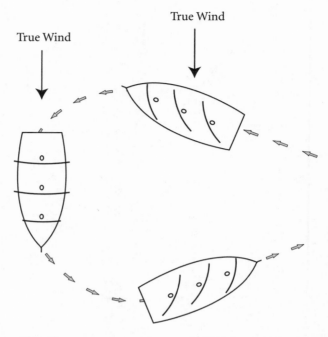

Figure 55. Jibing the square rig. Considered a foolproof maneuver for square sails.

boom and the sail immediately swing across to the opposite side of the vessel subjecting the sail, the mast supports (shrouds and stays), and the mast to a severe impact (fig. 57) that may rip the sail, break a shroud or stay, and even break the mast. The vessel may be rolled over, so that the mast(s) and sail(s) are in the water (a knockdown), or it may even capsize. If the boom is low enough, it could strike and severely injure a crew member or knock the person overboard. To minimize the danger of an accidental jibe, fore-and-aft-rigged vessels usually sail with the wind on the quarter and make a series of controlled jibes (jibing downwind); or they rig a preventer, a block-and-tackle arrangement that prevents the boom from swinging inboard (toward the center of the vessel).

POINTS OF A COMPASS

The *points of sail* are not to be confused with the *points of a compass*. In the days of sail, the circumference of a compass was divided into thirty-two

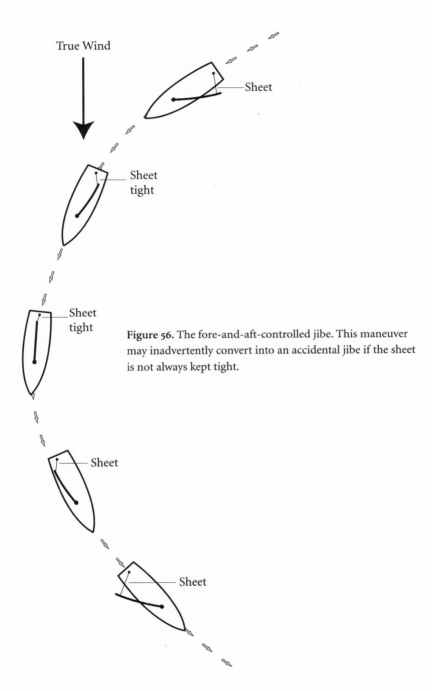

True Wind

Sheet

Sheet
tight

Sheet
tight

Sheet

Sheet

Figure 56. The fore-and-aft-controlled jibe. This maneuver may inadvertently convert into an accidental jibe if the sheet is not always kept tight.

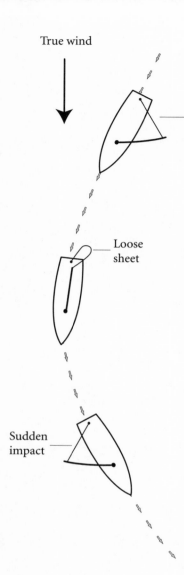

True wind

Sheet

Loose
sheet

Figure 57. The fore-and-aft accidental jibe.
This inadvertent movement is extremely
dangerous and may result in damage to sail,
rigging, mast, and may even cause a knockdown.

Sudden
impact

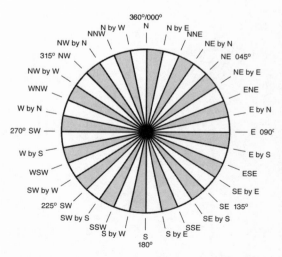

Figure 58. The points of a compass are shown
as they relate to 360 degrees.

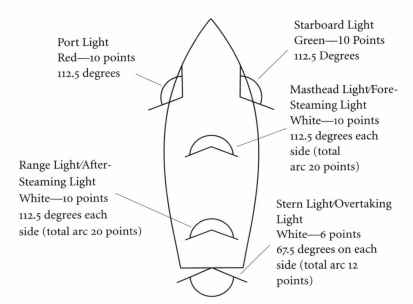

Port Light
Red—10 points
112.5 degrees

Starboard Light
Green—10 Points
112.5 Degrees

Masthead Light/Fore-
Steaming Light
White—10 points
112.5 degrees each
side (total
arc 20 points)

Range Light/After-
Steaming Light
White—10 points
112.5 degrees each
side (total arc 20 points)

Stern Light/Overtaking
Light
White—6 points
67.5 degrees on each
side (total arc 12
points)

Figure 59. Arcs of navigation lights. A sailing vessel does not show masthead lights unless it is under sail and power.

points, each of 11.25 degrees (360 divided by 32 equals 11.25). The cardinal points were North, East, South and West and the half cardinal points were Northeast, Southeast, Southwest and Northwest. The remaining points are shown on figure 58.

A seaman was required to box-the-compass; this consisted of reciting from memory all the points of the compass from North through East to North again and also from North through West and to North again. When a person was standing watch as helmsman, the course to steer was specified as one of these points. Later, when navigation became more precise, the point system was abandoned for steering, and the course was specified by degrees of the compass. The point system is still used, however, for specifying the arc of visibility of a vessel's navigation lights (fig. 59), and it is sometimes still used by lookouts to report the relative bearing of an object; for example, "Ship bearing two points on the starboard bow" or "a point abaft the port beam."

9

Sail
Area
Adjustments

When the wind velocity increases, it is often necessary to reduce sail area keep the vessel on course; a high wind force on the sail or sails can create a turning effect that cannot be corrected by rudder action. Also, it may be necessary to reduce sail area to prevent capsizing.

REDUCING SAIL AREA

The force on the sail generated by the wind is proportional to the increase in wind velocity squared. That is, when the wind velocity doubles from six knots to twelve knots, the force on the sail is four times greater than the initial wind force at six knots. The effective sail area may be reduced by

1. replacing a large sail with a smaller sail; on today's typical fore-and-aft vessels, for example, the large genoa is usually replaced with a smaller jib;
2. taking down (removing) one or more sails; on a cutter, for example, one of the headsails can be removed;
3. furling the sail, that is, folding it and tying it to its yard or boom;
4. reducing the effective area of a sail.

Figure 60. Brails for sail area reduction. The Greeks and Romans used this method to reduce sail area.

The initial scheme for reducing the area of a sail was the use of *brails*. They were developed possibly as early as the second millennium B.C. and used by the Romans, Greeks, and Byzantines.[1] A brail was a line attached to the yard that passed through a vertical line of rings attached to the sail. When the brail was tightened, the bottom of the sail was raised toward the yard arm, thereby reducing sail area (fig. 60). The yard could then be lowered. This method of reducing sail area had advantages over the later method of reefing square sails. Brail reefing could be accomplished from deck level;[2] in a heavy blow lowering the sail could reduce the overturning effect that causes a vessel to heel, and possibly capsize. The brail method, however, was practical only for a single square sail and was not feasible for square-riggers where square sails were located one above the other.

The next system for reducing sail area used a horizontal strip of sailcloth laced to the foot of the sail called a bonnet. Under high wind conditions, the bonnet was removed to make the sail smaller (fig. 61). Bonnets were used on the single-square-sail cogs in the twelfth or thirteenth century.

Reefing was introduced in the eighteenth century and is still in use today.

Figure 61. The bonnet for sail area reduction. This method was popular with the Vikings to reduce sail area on their longships.

On a square sail, reef points (short lengths of line attached to the sail) were positioned below the yard and parallel to it. Some sails were equipped with two or three sets of reef points. To reduce sail area, crewmen standing on footropes attached to the yard pulled the sail up until the reef points could be tied around the yard (fig. 62). On fore-and-aft sails, reef points are located in horizontal rows some distance above the boom. To reef the sail, it is first lowered until the reef points are level with the boom. The reef points are then tied about the boom, or under the sail, and the halyard is tightened to take the slack out of the reefed sail (fig. 63). Reefing a fore-and-aft sail is a much safer and usually faster procedure than what is required for a square sail as it does not require crewmen to go aloft. Jibs and staysails can be reefed in the same manner, but it is usually more desirable to remove the jib or staysail, or replace it with a smaller sail.

INCREASING SAIL AREA

Under conditions where there is an extremely light wind or breeze, it may be desirable to increase sail area. Studding sails (pronounced stunsails) were in common use on square-riggers for this purpose but could only be used when the wind was from abaft the beam and were usually set only on the windward side, unless the vessel was sailing directly downwind. The studding sail consisted

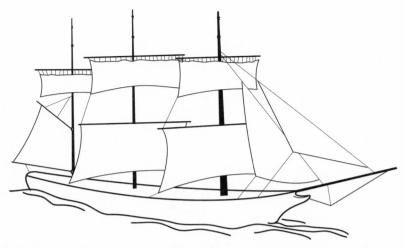

Figure 62. Square fore and main topsails reefed and yards lowered. Some cautious captains would furl the upper sails at nightfall.

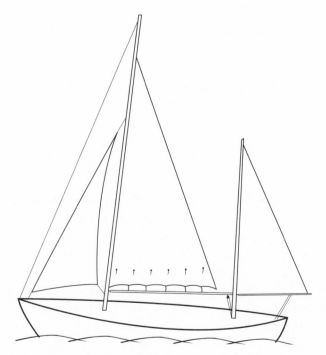

Figure 63. Single-reefed fore-and-aft mainsail. This is the common method of reefing on today's yachts.

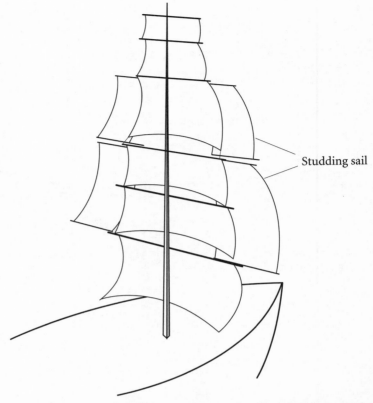

Studding sail

Figure 64. Studding sails. These sails are only used on the windward side, except when the wind is directly from astern.

of a vertical strip of sailcloth suspended from a boom that was temporarily attached to the end of a yardarm (fig. 64). Studding sails have been in continuous use on square-riggers since the sixteenth century.[3]

It was the studding sail that allowed Admiral Nelson to defeat the combined French and Spanish fleet at the Battle of Trafalgar (1805), an event that thwarted Napoleon's planned invasion of England. In the summer of 1805, Napoleon's invasion force comprised 120,000 troops and 2,343 craft and boats; but the fleet that was to protect this invasion force was in Cadiz, almost a thousand miles away. The invasion was postponed until the following spring, and the combined French and Spanish fleets, under Admiral Villeneuve, were ordered into the Mediterranean.[4] Before reaching Gibraltar, however, Villeneuve sighted Nelson's fleet. In order not to risk his ships in battle, Villeneuve ordered them to form a single line heading north toward Cadiz. The wind was very light and from the west, providing Villeneuve with a beam wind, a good point of sail for maximum speed in light wind. Nelson was west of Villeneuve, however, and was forced to sail downwind (a poor point of sail) to catch the enemy; at 6:05 A.M. Nelson ordered the British fleet to set all possible sail.[5] The French-Spanish fleet consisted of thirty-three ships of the line and included the four-decker *Santissima Trinidad,* the largest and—with 138 guns—most heavily armed ship in the world. Nelson's fleet of twenty-seven ships formed into two squadrons and attacked to cross Villeneuve's line. The largest British squadron, under Vice Adm. Cuthbert Collingwood, engaged Villeneuve's rear sixteen ships; then Nelson—after signaling his famous message, "England expects that every man will do his duty"—with twelve ships attacked the center of Villeneuve's line. The British ships, sailing directly downwind with studding sails set on both sides, were able to break through and shatter the French admiral's defenses. The battle ended about 5:00 P.M. with Villeneuve losing eighteen ships. Sadly, Nelson would not be able to savor the great victory because he was shot and killed during the battle.[6] When Nelson defeated the French-Spanish fleet at Trafalgar, Napoleon had lost control of the sea. His defeats at Moscow and Waterloo were, according to Mahan, "the inevitable consequence of Trafalgar."[7] The British victory during the Napoleonic Wars is the second incident in maritime history in which control of the sea determined the outcome of a major land war.[8]

On the fore-and-aft rigged vessels, sail area can be increased using a large, basically triangular sail called the spinnaker. It is used primarily for sailing downwind, but under certain conditions it is also set on a beam reach. The spinnaker is positioned ahead of the forestay, and the lower outboard corner is supported by a temporary horizontal boom attached to the mast (fig. 65). The sail was first introduced on British cruising and racing yachts in 1870[9] and later was sometimes used on Pacific lumber schooners.[10] The spinnaker is currently used on racing yachts because a large crew is required to set the sail and tend it. Recently, a *cruising spinnaker* (also known as an *asymmetrical spinnaker*) was developed for cruising yachts. Because it is not supported by a temporary boom, it requires a smaller crew, but it is a much less effective sail for sailing directly downwind than the true symmetrical spinnaker.

According to the *Oxford English Dictionary,* the word *spinnaker* originated as "a fanciful formation on spinx, mispronunciation of *Sphinx,* the

Figure 65. The spinnaker. Typically, this sail is used only on racing yachts as a large crew is required to manage it.

name of the first yacht [that] commonly carried the sail." Another story credits a crew member of the yacht *Niobe* for coining the word. After setting this newly developed balloonlike sail, he is said to have commented, "That ought to make her spin [go fast]." The *Niobe,* in June 1866, was purportedly the first yacht to fly this sail, which ultimately became known as a spinmaker and later spinnaker.[11]

10

Schooners

"I like the way she schoons!" At a launching this was the statement of a spectator who was impressed with the way the vessel glided across the water. The ship's owner then exclaimed, "A schooner let her be!"

The word *schoon* could have been related to the Scottish verb *to scoon* that implied skipping over the water like a flat stone;[1] or it could have come from the sixteenth-century Dutch word *scoon,* meaning beautiful, fair, or lovely.[2] The incident described here purportedly occurred in Gloucester in 1713, and the name *schooner* was to continue to describe a two-masted fore-and-aft-rigged vessel on which the aftermast was the mainmast. However, smaller craft rigged in this manner continued to be called shallops because they were in use on both sides of the Atlantic long before 1713. Also, the English insisted on calling a large-decked schooner a sloop as late as 1750.[3] Later, the designation of a vessel as a schooner also included fore-and-aft-rigged vessels with three or more masts.

The basic schooner sail arrangement derived from the Dutch conversion during the fifteenth and sixteenth centuries of the lateen sail into a true fore-and-aft sail; the schooner rig was perfected and implemented by Americans, however, beginning in the area around Gloucester, Massachusetts, where the

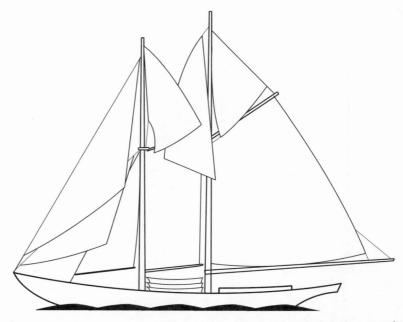

Figure 66. The Gloucester fishing schooner. The individual fishing dories are nested and stored on deck.

first seagoing schooner was built in 1713. She was designed for fishing the Grand Banks and returning rapidly to port. By 1721 there were 120 fishing schooners operating out of the Marblehead area, and this number increased to 160 in 1731.[4] Eventually, this Gloucester-type of fishing schooner was built throughout New England and also into Nova Scotia. The rig consisted of gaff-rigged sails on the foremast and mainmast with a fore-and-aft topsail above the gaff, jibs, and staysails. The main boom overhung the stern to obtain a maximum mainsail area.[5] When wind conditions permitted, a fisherman's staysail was set. This was a large four-sided sail set high from the top of the mainmast. Some schooners carried a large staysail between the mainmast and the foremast instead of a gaffed foresail; they were called staysail schooners. At first fishing was by means of hand lines from the schooner's deck, but later as the schooners became larger, line fishing was from dories. Dories were small flat-bottom rowing boats constructed with sloping sides so that they could be stacked (nested) one within the other on the deck of the schooner.

The Gloucester fishing schooner and the dory fishermen were immortalized in Killing's classic *Captains Courageous,* which was made into a

Figure 67. The Baltimore clipper schooner. This vessel was the preferred privateering vessel of the War of 1812 because of its exceptional windward performance.

Hollywood movie in the 1930s. These schooners remained active commercial-fishing vessels well into the 1900s, and fisherman's cup races were conducted in the 1920s and 1930s to promote continuing interest in these classic vessels. The most frequent winner was the Nova Scotia–built *Bluenose*. A replica of the original *Bluenose* was built in 1963.[6] The Gloucester fishing schooner illustrated in figure 66, also known as the Grand Banks schooner, was made obsolete not by steam but by the internal combustion engine.[7]

By 1750 two types of schooners were in use in America, the large ocean-going schooner used for coastal voyages and deep-sea fishing and a smaller craft for inshore work. These smaller vessels were usually decked and were called shallops. The shallops carried two gaff-rigged sails of roughly equal size but no bowsprit or jibs. The foremast was stepped well forward in the bow. The British built similar vessels rigged in the same manner, but their shallops were usually smaller (about twenty-five feet) and often without a deck. Vessels rigged in this manner became known as bald-headed schooners and presently "bald-headed" pertains to a fore-and-aft rigged vessel that is not flying a headsail (jib or staysail).[8] "Bald-headed" has also been used to describe a Bermuda-rigged schooner (no gaff topsail).[9]

Initially, the British preferred the single-mast cutter rig for their small fast vessels, but the cutter rig was not suitable for a larger vessel because the sails became too heavy to hoist. At this time, the American schooners were gaining a reputation for speed and seaworthiness. In 1757 the British purchased a 130-ton schooner built in Virginia; it was the first schooner registered in the Royal Navy. Six additional Marblehead schooners were acquired between the years 1767 and 1768, and two more were built for the Royal Navy in New York in 1767. Some English cutters were converted into schooners by cutting the hull in half, moving the halves apart ten or fifteen feet, and then constructing a new center hull section. This extended hull was then rigged as a two-masted schooner.[10]

Fast schooners were also built in Virginia and in the Chesapeake Bay area. The Virginia pilot boat was thirty-five to forty-five feet in length with a deep keel aft and raked masts. The foot of the gaffed mainsail was attached to a boom, but the gaffed foresail was not. They also set a large main-topmast stay-sail, and the bowsprit carried a large jib.[11] The Chesapeake Bay schooners were much larger. By 1757 some were eighty feet long, mounted fourteen guns, and were known as Baltimore clipper schooners (the first ones were built in 1751). These vessels were exceptionally fast topsail schooners because of the narrow beam, vast sail area, and the square sail (topsail) on the foremast (fig. 67).

Due to their speed and excellent windward performance, these schooners were the preferred vessels for privateering against British merchant ships during the War of 1812. Captured schooners, which by this time had attained a length of 115 feet and speeds of ten to twelve knots under optimum wind conditions, were often taken into the Royal Navy.[12] After the war of 1812, the Baltimore clipper schooners could not function competitively as cargo vessels due to their small cargo hold. Two of them were taken into the United States Navy; others were employed as revenue cutters; some became slavers and South American privateers.[13] The Baltimore clipper schooners were also used as pilot boats to dash out and put pilots aboard incoming ships.

The slave trade started after Columbus's discovery, and the slave ship could be any type of ship that was available. The slave trade was outlawed by the United States and Great Britain in 1807, and after termination of the War of 1812 American and British navy ships were available to pursue slave ships. A fast slave ship was required to outsail a pursuing man-of-war. The slavers used the Baltimore clipper schooners for this purpose, but the United States Navy

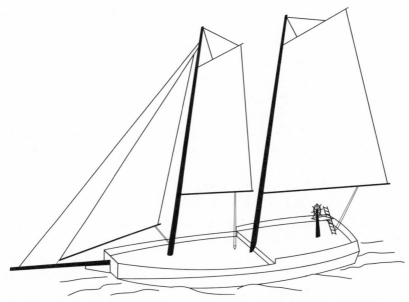

Figure 68. The San Francisco Bay scow schooner. The elevated wheel and pulpit permitted the helmsman to see over the cargo that was stored on deck.

also used these fast schooners to run the slavers down.[14] The basic hull design of the Baltimore clipper schooner was later adopted for America's fast square-rigged clipper ships. The *Pride of Baltimore II,* completed in 1988, is a replica of a typical Baltimore clipper topsail schooner and serves as a goodwill sailing ambassador for the city and the state of Maryland. The original *Pride of Baltimore* was tragically lost at sea in 1986.[15]

The New England coastal schooners were mostly rigged with only fore-and-aft sails, but square topsails were added for vessels sailing to the West Indies. Schooners in Great Britain and on the Continent usually were equipped with square sails on the foremast so that in Europe the term schooner automatically implied a vessel with square sails. If square sails were absent, the term fore-and-aft schooner was used to denote the absence of square sails. Conversely, in America the term schooner denoted fore-and-aft sails only; with square sails the vessel was called a topsail schooner. Studding sails were common to increase the area of the square sails until the end of the 1870s.[16] The British equipped some schooners with four square-sails on the foremast in addition to the typical fore-and-aft foresails. These vessels were known as schooner brigantines and were popular from about 1820 to 1880.

The schooner brigantines were a good balance between the square and the fore-and-aft rig. The vessels could sail as close to the wind as a true schooner; but with the wind from the quarter or from astern, there were four additional square sails that could be augmented by studding sails. The large sail area on this vessel was extremely effective in making fast passages.

There were also variations in hull design to meet special conditions. Seagoing and Pacific Coast schooners were built with deep keels; but the New England schooners that were required to operate in shallow waters and adjacent to sand bars and other obstructions were equipped with centerboards. For operation in high tidal areas the schooners had flat bottoms to permit them to sit on the bottom during low tide. These vessels were normally not equipped with centerboards as mud would tend to clog about the centerboard and make it inoperable. A keel-type vessel would lie on its side at low tide, and the mud suction on the hull had a tendency to keep the vessel in this heeled position as the tide was rising, creating a danger of flooding.[17] In the San Francisco Bay area, a scow schooner was developed for the shallow tributaries that flowed into San Francisco Bay. The scow schooner had an exceptionally shallow draft, a square (transom) bow, and a *helm pulpit*, a raised platform on which the helm was located to permit the helmsman to see over the cargo (usually bales of hay) stored on deck (fig. 68).[18]

The American coastal trade needed larger schooners after 1850 to carry coal and lumber; forty-four three-masted schooners of three hundred tons and larger were constructed in 1850 to 1860. Three-masted schooners without square sails and with masts of equal height were known as *tern* schooners or terns, the word meaning three of a kind. The first four-master was built in 1880 and this rig became popular for vessels of 180 to 240 feet long.[19] The *Thomas W. Lawson,* built in Quincy, Massachusetts, in 1890, had seven masts and was believed to be the largest schooner ever built; she was 385 feet long. Each of the seven masts was identical and consisted of a 135-foot steel lower mast and a 58-foot pine topmast. All halyards, topping lifts, and sheets were led to two large steam winches, one located under the forecastle and the other in the afterdeck house. There were four smaller winches for handling cargo and hoisting the topsails. The steam winches permitted a crew of sixteen. The ship was lost in heavy weather off the Scilly Islands in 1907 with either all hands or possibly one survivor.[20] The *Thomas W. Lawson* was a ship that straddled the new mechanical age and the old Age of Sail.

For over two centuries, ocean commerce was carried out in square-rigged vessels; but after 1840, brigs, barks, and ships became less popular in the

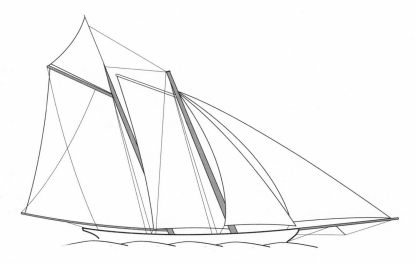

Figure 69. The schooner yacht *American.* The foresail overlaps the mainsail on this vessel, the winner of Great Britain's Hundred Guinea Cup—which became the America's Cup.

American coastal trade. Schooners were cheaper to rig than square-riggers because the fore-and-aft rig did not require the square-riggers' numerous spars (yards) and complex rigging. Also, schooners were more economical to operate; a smaller crew was required because the fore-and-aft sails could be raised and lowered from deck level as opposed to the square sails that required seamen to climb aloft to set and furl them. Frequently, the schooner could sail a shorter route because fore-and-aft sails could be trimmed to sail closer to the direction of the true wind. This also allowed schooners to be worked into and out of harbors and rivers more easily than the square-rigged vessels.

By 1854 schooners had become extremely popular in Europe for coastal commerce. They carried fruit from the Azores and Mediterranean to London and even pineapples from the West Indies. Schooners were in regular trade around the coastline of the British Islands and into ports on the Continent. They were also used in some deep-water trade routes carrying salt cod from Newfoundland and made the long and dangerous voyage around Cape Horn to bring copper ore from Chile.[21] Square-rigged vessels continued to be used for long voyages, particularly along trade-wind routes, where the greater sail area of the square-riggers gave them a speed advantage.

The advent of steam permitted schooners to operate with a smaller crew; a donkey boiler and a steam-powered winch could be used to raise the heavy sails and to operate the anchor windlass. As late as 1882 it was much more economical to ship lumber and coal by means of a six-hundred-ton three-masted schooner than by a steam-powered ship. World War I created a great need for shipping and many three-masted schooners were constructed between 1916 and 1920. The last three-masted schooner was constructed in 1929 at Essex, Massachusetts.[22]

Today many cruising yachts and all racing yachts use the genoa jib (introduced in 1927) to obtain the overlapping-sail slot effect that enhances the windward performance of fore-and-aft sails; this concept was developed much earlier, however, on the American schooners.

The schooner yacht *America* was built in New York in 1851 to compete in the race around the Isle of Wight in the English Channel, sponsored by the Royal Yacht Squadron. The *America* was a two-masted schooner: the foot of the mainsail was attached to a boom, but the foot of the foresail was not, and it overlapped the luff of the mainsail (fig. 69).[23] This sail arrangement was similar to that used on the Virginia pilot boat schooners. Queen Victoria of England watched the race, and toward the end she and her signal-master had the following conversation:

"Say, signal-master, are the yachts in sight?"
"Yes, may it please Your Majesty."
"Which is first?"
"The *America.*"
"Which is second?"
"Ah, Your Majesty, there is no second."[24]

The *America* won the race and the Hundred Guinea Cup that later became known as the America's Cup.

This overlapping foresail-mainsail arrangement was also used on American revenue cutters in the 1800s. Today this specific rig can be seen on the *Californian,* a topsail schooner that is a replica of the *L. W. Lawrence,* a revenue cutter that was wrecked near the entrance to San Francisco Bay in 1850. The *Californian* was launched in San Diego in 1984 and is operated by the Nautical Heritage Society of San Clemente, California. The *Californian,* homeported in Long Beach, is used for youth training programs in Pacific Coast ports.

Prior to 1700 schooners were used mainly for pleasure. Now, after almost three centuries of carrying every conceivable cargo, serving as privateers and warships, inland lake and river craft, fishermen, pilot vessels, and school ships, the schooner has reverted back to her original role of a recreational vessel. But the American schooners remained viable commercial vessels for over two hundred years (1713 to 1920); and within this relatively short period, the schooners, along with the fast American clippers and the nimble and devastating USS *Constitution*–type Joshua Humphreys frigates, earned for America its impressive nautical heritage.[25]

11

The Reign
of the
Clipper Ship

Surprisingly, the introduction of the steam engine for marine propulsion did not immediately trigger the demise of the sailing ships. On the contrary, steam-powered sidewheel tugs appeared in the early 1800s and eliminated the need for ships to maneuver under sail to get in and out of port. Sailing ships could now be designed for optimum performance at sea.[1] These ships became known as clipper ships (fig. 70) because they sailed at a fast clip; however, the term clipper was earlier applied to the Baltimore-built fast schooners popular with American privateers during the War of 1812.

The first prototype, the *Ann McKimm*, was built in 1832 in Baltimore, utilizing the hull of a large Baltimore clipper schooner but with a ship rig. The *Ann McKimm* was not considered a true clipper: she had a wider beam than later clippers; the keel sloped down from eleven feet to seventeen feet; and although the bow was sharper than conventional ships of that era, it was not as sharp as later clippers.[2] The *Ann McKimm* proved to be faster than the square-rigged ships of her time and was considered to be a great success.

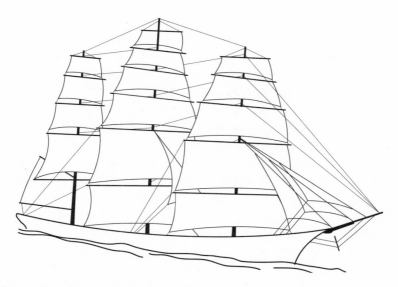

Figure 70. The clipper ship. With its multitude of sails to catch and harness the wind, the clipper was the fastest cargo-carrying sailing ship ever.

CLIPPER DESIGNS

"Cod's head and mackerel tail" was the way many described the hull shape of a preclipper merchant ship. This implied that the bow should be rounded (like a cod's head) to provide buoyancy for the bow to ride up over oncoming waves, and the stern should be narrow (like a mackerel tail) for minimum visible turbulence. John Wilks Griffiths, an American ship designer, conducted tank tests of various hull shapes and studied the performance of the *Ann McKimm*. He resolved that the bow should be sharp to cut through the oncoming waves and the hull long and narrow; but the fin like a mackerel tail caused an invisible suction that slowed down the vessel. Instead, the stern should have a fuller shape.[3] The ship built to John Wilks Griffiths's design was the *Rainbow,* the first true clipper. The *Rainbow* was built in New York in 1845[4] and was even a greater success than the *Ann McKimm.* The *Rainbow* was a much larger ship and therefore could carry a larger cargo and attained about twice the speed of conventional preclipper ships.

Although the first true clipper ship was built in New York, it was in Boston that the clipper attained its ultimate perfection, particularly the ships designed and built by Donald McKay. He was born in Shelburne, Nova Scotia, in 1810;

emigrated to New York; and was employed in the shipyard of Isaac Web; here McKay quickly mastered the profession and later moved to Boston. He was a self-taught genius and his ships were so successful that owners frequently allowed him to name the ships he constructed. The *Stag Hound, Mastiff, Flying Cloud, Flying Fish, Westward Ho,* and *Sovereign of the Seas* were some of his extremely fast and successful clipper ships. His *Lightning* was reputed to be the fastest sailing-ship ever built and records conclusively show that Donald McKay was the supreme designer and builder of clipper ships.[5]

Nat Palmer was another successful pioneer of clipper ship design. Unlike John Wilks Griffiths and Donald McKay, Nat Palmer went to sea at age fourteen and rapidly advanced to become a master mariner. In 1833 he became the captain of the *Huntsville,* a packet that was constructed with a unique U-shaped hull; at that time ship designers believed that a V-shaped bottom was the preferred shape. In his first voyage on the *Huntsville* Palmer reduced the sailing time from New Orleans to New York from eighteen to fourteen days. Later, he not only commanded packets on the New York–Liverpool run but contributed to their design, utilizing his experience at sea and specifying the U-shaped hull.

On a return voyage from China, Nat Palmer formulated a concept for a faster ship that would have a greater spread of sails, a long narrow hull, and a flat (U-shaped) bottom. The flat bottom, in addition to providing more cargo space, would allow the vessel to ride over the incoming seas instead of plowing through them. The ship built to his design was the *Hougua* and was completed before the *Rainbow.* In her first voyage from New England to Hong Kong, the *Hougua* established a record of 84 days. A year and a half earlier it had taken Captain Palmer 111 days to make the same crossing in the packet *Paul Jones.*[6]

Nat Palmer designed several fast clippers and in 1850 his *Oriental* was the first clipper to sail into London after a ninety-seven-day passage from Hong Kong. The British ship *Jeanette* left China three days earlier and arrived in London forty-seven days after the *Oriental.* The British ship designers were extremely impressed; they examined the *Oriental,* took notes, made quick sketches; and as the London *Times* reported, "We must run a race with our gigantic and unshackled rival."[7]

The remarkable speed attained by the clippers was due to the following design features:

1. The sharp bow minimized resistance by cutting through the oncoming seas; the concave shape of the bow above the waterline (presently known as a *clipper bow*) was suggested by a model of a Singapore sampan;[8]

2. The stern was constructed rounder than on preclipper vessels; this contributed to speed by minimizing the surface of the hull that was in contact
   with the water.

3. The length-to-beam ratio was increased to about six to one, resulting in a long
   narrow hull that permitted construction of the sharp bow, and the entire
   length maximized speed; the limiting speed (the hull speed) of a displacement
   hull is proportional to the square root of the waterline length of the vessel (a
   displacement hull—as opposed to a flat or modified V-shaped planing hull—
   achieves its buoyancy, or flotation capacity, by displacing a volume of water
   equal in weight to the hull and its load);[9] a vessel with a longer displacement
   hull will be faster than a shorter displacement-hull vessel, provided there is
   sufficient power to overcome the resistance of the water and air.

4. The main deck was constructed flush with minimum-height cabin superstructure to minimize wind resistance.

Preclipper ships of that era were typically equipped with a maximum of six
square sails located one above the other. To obtain a greater sail area, some
clipper ships were fitted with taller masts (thirteen stories high) that allowed
a seventh sail, the moon sail (moonraker), and even an eighth sail—a
stargazer.[10] Jibs were positioned over the bowsprit and staysails on the many
fore-and-aft mast supports (stays) to provide a maximum sail area. Studding
sails were also used. A large crew was required to handle this tremendous
expanse of sail. Most clippers were rigged as three- or four-masted full-rigged
ships, but some were four-masted barks. The fourth mast was called the
spanker mast.

DEMAND FOR FAST SHIPS

The end in China of the Opium War in 1842 ceded Hong Kong to Britain and
opened five other ports to foreign commerce, instigating the profitable China
tea trade. Tea from China was in great demand, but the voyage from China
to Europe in a preclipper required six months, so long that the tea would
begin to mildew. Clippers reduced shipping time from six to three months.

   The discovery of gold in California and Australia created an additional
demand for fast ships. Prospective miners anxious to get to the gold fields were
willing to pay the high cost of passage in clipper ships. East Coast merchants
could justify high shipping costs in order to expedite shipment of their goods
to the gold camps where prices for trade goods were astronomical. In 1850 the

clipper *Samuel Russell* delivered a cargo to San Francisco that was worth $275,000, which was four times the construction cost of the ship; ninety-seven days earlier in New York the cargo cost $84,626.[11] The construction and operation of clipper ships was an extremely profitable venture. One voyage would pay for the cost of the ship, and subsequent voyages were almost pure profit. Twenty new clippers were built in 1850; 40 in 1851; 66 in 1852; and 125 in 1853.[12]

The maximum speed of a preclipper merchant sailing ship was about ten knots, and a few could average six knots on a voyage; 150 miles was considered an excellent day's run. The American clippers routinely made runs of 250 miles a day and attained speeds of eighteen to twenty knots.[13] The performance attained by the clippers was remarkable. In 1854 the *Lightning* sailed 436 miles in twenty-four hours maintaining a speed of eighteen to eighteen and a half knots.[14] The *James Baines* at one time attained a speed of twenty-one knots during a run of 420 miles in one day.[15] The all-time record for a sailing ship for a voyage from New York to Liverpool, established by the *Sovereign of the Seas*, was thirteen days and fourteen hours, attaining a speed of twenty-two knots.[16] The *Champion of the Seas* in 1854 logged a run of 465 nautical miles in one day— an average speed of 19.375 knots for a one-day run.[17] In 1848 the *Sea Witch* sailed from Hong Kong to New York in seventy-four days. This record has never been bettered by a sailing ship.[18] In 1851 the *Flying Cloud* sailed 17,597 nautical miles from New York to San Francisco around Cape Horn in eighty-nine days and twenty-one hours, with an average speed of over eight knots.[19] The only sailing vessel to beat *Flying Cloud*'s record to San Francisco was a schooner that sailed the shorter route through the Straits of Magellan.

The consistent high-speed performance of the clippers was authenticated by the famous Tea Clipper Race of 1866 in which five clipper ships raced from China to England. The five ships were the *Ariel, Taeping, Serica, Fiery Cross,* and *Taitsin.* The race started at the Pagoda Anchorage at Foochow, China, and ended at the London dock, a distance of sixteen thousand miles. The first three ships to finish were the *Taeping, Ariel,* and the *Serica;* the three clippers arrived in the Thames on the same tide and docked in London within two hours of each other. Their total time for the voyage was ninety-nine days, a record that has never been beaten. The other two ships arrived in London two days later.[20] Steam ships did not attain these speeds until thirty years later.[21]

INCREASING SIZE AND SPEED

The largest American clipper, built for the New York–San Francisco trade, was the *Great Republic* (designed by Donald McKay), a four-masted barque, 325

feet in length and a beam of 53 feet. Unfortunately, it was not possible to eval-
uate her performance because she was partially destroyed by fire while she was
being fitted-out for her maiden voyage. As a result, her hull and rig were cut
down to more modest proportions.[22]

Eventually, England recognized the exceptional performance of the clipper
ships and began a building program that produced extremely fast ones. The
Thermopylae, built in England in 1868, sailed from London to Melbourne in
fifty-nine days and was reputed to be the fastest clipper ship.[23] The *Cutty Sark,*
also built in England, was *Thermopylae*'s primary rival in the China tea trade
and is now on display, fully restored, in Greenwich, England.

Steel spars and rigging were introduced in 1863, but iron-hulled ships were
built earlier in the 1800s. The use of iron reduced the weight of the hull by
about one-third, but iron hulls were used mostly for steamships. For sailing
ships, wood remained the preferred material. Copper sheathing was sometimes used to protect the wood from marine growth that reduced the speed
of the ship. In 1840 an alloy of copper and zinc, called *yellow metal,* was used
for sheathing; it lasted for as long as ten years. Copper or the yellow metal
alloy could not be used on iron hulls because of the galvanic corrosion
between the iron and copper or yellow metal.[24] There was no way to protect
iron hulls from the accumulation of marine growth until the introduction
of copper-based antifouling paint in 1870.[25] To take advantage of the weight
reduction available by using iron and the resistance to marine growth by using
yellow metal, the British developed what came to be known as a composite
hull. The ship's frames, deck beams, and other internal structures were made
of iron and the external planking was wood, lined with yellow metal. Both the
Thermopylae and the *Cutty Sark* were composite-hull clippers.[26]

The speed attained by these clipper ships was due to (1) the design of the
hull, (2) a massive sail area, and (3) an aggressive captain who was anxious
to set records and would carry sail under high-wind conditions in which pru-
dent skippers would shorten sail. When rounding the Horn, most skippers
would not only reduce sail but at times lower upper yards when weather conditions were extreme. Most clipper captains carried all sail possible to maxi-
mize speed. Sail area was reduced only when the wind and seas created a dangerous condition.

CHARTS FOR WIND AND CURRENT

But there was one other contributor to the fast voyages attained by the clipper ships, Matthew Fontane Maury. He was an American naval officer who

devoted his studies to navigation and oceanography. Eventually he was appointed superintendent of the Depot of Charts and Instruments in 1842.[27] The logs and diaries of many ships were stored at the depot, and this appointment gave him the opportunity to study them. His studies allowed him to identify areas of steady winds and calm belts about which he once wrote, "The calm belts of the sea, like mountains on the land, stand mightily in the way of the voyager, but, like the mountains on the land, they have their passes and gaps."[28]

In 1847 and 1848 he published *Wind and Current Charts of the North Atlantic* and *Abstract Log for the Use of American Navigators*—what became known as "Sailing Directions"—and issued revised editions in 1850 and 1851.[29] These Sailing Directions included charts that identified areas of steady winds and calm belts, which mariners of all nations studied enthusiastically since the charts made possible considerable savings in voyage time. As the clipper ship era coincided with Maury's publications, captains of clippers took advantage of this extremely valuable information, and the Sailing Directions were a major factor in setting their voyage records.

At the start of the Civil War, Maury (a native of Virginia) resigned from the United States Navy and accepted a commission as a commander in the Confederate Navy. He experimented with electric mines and was later sent to England where, because of his international reputation, he was expected to be influential in procuring ships for the Confederate Navy; however, he was not notably successful. After the Civil War he served the Mexican government as commissioner of immigration. Later he was a professor at the Virginia Military Institute.[30] The United States Navy, remaining cognizant of his achievement in publishing the several editions of Sailing Directions, named a destroyer after him in 1939, the USS *Maury* (DD-401).[31] The clipper ship era lasted from 1845 to 1870 or perhaps another ten years to 1880. It ended due to the opening of the Suez Canal in 1868,[32] which cut the route to China by about four thousand miles and permitted steamships to obtain coal en route. It is ironic that the canal opened just one week before the launching of the *Cutty Sark,* one of the most famous clippers.

Only in recent years have today's high-performance racing yachts been able to equal the performance of clipper ships in routes around Cape Horn. Yet, the racing yachts have the advantage of improved materials for sails, rigging, and hull construction that were not available a hundred years ago. Also, racing yachts receive weather reports by radio to determine the location of optimum wind conditions—and the racing yachts carry no cargo. There is no doubt that the clipper ships were the fastest and grandest cargo-carrying sailing vessels of all time. And, according to Samuel Eliot Morison, among the most memorable, "for one who has sailed a clipper ship, even in fancy, all later modes of ocean carriage must seem decadent."[33]

The down-easter was the sequel to the clipper ship and appeared about the time that steamers started to supersede the clippers. The down-easters were ship rigged and wooden hulled, and they had the same clean lines as the clippers. They were not as fast as the clippers but had great cargo capacity. They were called down-easters because they were built *down east* of Boston in the Maine to New Hampshire area, where lumber for hull construction was plentiful; this allowed them to compete economically with the iron-hulled clippers and steamers until the end of the century.[34] Some naval historians contend that the down-easter was the finest all-around merchant sailing ship ever built.[35]

12

*W*eatherliness

Douglas Philips-Birt points out that "the battle to sail to windward efficiently has daunted seamen since the dawn of maritime history."[1] This chapter takes a look at that battle: how it is waged by modern sailors and how it was waged in the past.

Weatherliness is the ability of a vessel to sail to weather, the direction from which the wind is blowing. Today, *pointing* is the term used to describe a vessel's ability to sail against the wind. The vessel that can sail closest to the direction from which the wind is blowing is said to point higher or to *outpoint* the other vessels.

Nowadays, high pointing is of prime importance only to racing sailboats. But in the days of sail, a vessel's ability to sail close to the wind could significantly reduce the distance sailed during a voyage. For example, imagine two vessels sailing to windward at the same speed: one vessel pointing 4.25 points (47.8 degrees) and the other vessel pointing only 5.25 points (59.1 degrees). After twenty minutes the latter vessel would be four minutes behind. Also, in beating to windward twenty miles, a vessel pointing 4.25 points (47.8 degrees) would travel 32 miles and a vessel sailing at 4 points (45.0 degrees) would travel 28.3 miles.[2]

High pointing also enhances a vessel's ability to maneuver in and out of port. Before the advent of steam-powered sidewheel tugs in the early 1800s, the only means of towing a ship was with rowing boats that could not always provide

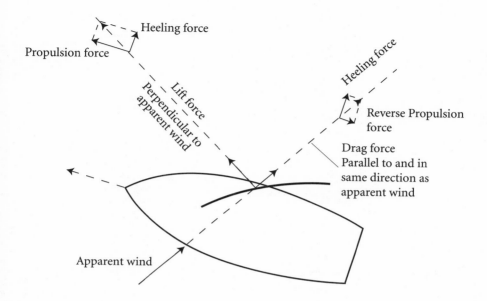

Figure 71. Sail trimmed for lift. The objective is to trim the sail for maximum lift and minimum drag.

enough power against a strong wind or tidal current. Kedging was an alternative; it involved setting an anchor by boat in the desired direction, and then working the ship up to it by hauling in on the anchor line. This procedure frequently had to be repeated several times.[3] Sailing ships sometimes had to lay offshore until favorable wind or tidal current allowed them to proceed into port.

Typically sailing ships would leave port at the time of the morning ebb tide to take advantage of the morning land breeze that occurs in many coastal areas. Because the land cools more quickly than the sea after the sun sets, the air over the land becomes heavier than the air over the water and flows out to sea, creating a land breeze (the land breeze–sea breeze effect). Usually this land breeze continues through the early morning.[4]

LIFT

When a vessel sails downwind, the wind produces a force against the sail that pushes the vessel in the downwind direction; but for sailing across the wind and against the wind, the sail must be positioned so that the apparent wind

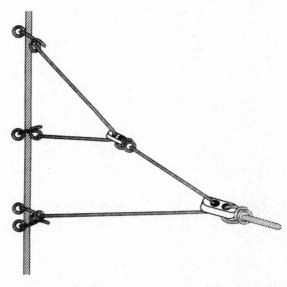

Figure 72. Bowline and three-point bridle. This arrangement minimized the curl of the luff.

strikes the leading edge of the sail at an acute angle. The conventional method of visualizing the two forces resulting from the apparent wind striking the leading edge of the sail at an acute angle is to segregate the forces into a *lift* (the good) force and a *drag* (the bad) force. The direction of the lift force is perpendicular to the apparent wind; the direction of the drag force is parallel to the apparent wind.[5] When the lift and drag forces acting on the sail are further segregated into fore-and-aft and athwartship (side-to-side) components, the lift force becomes a propulsion force and a heeling force. The drag force becomes an additional heeling force and a reverse propulsion force. The net forces, propulsion and heeling, are shown in figure 71. The heeling forces are opposed by the lateral resistance of the keel and the underwater portion of the hull. The net propulsion force drives the vessel in the ahead direction.

Nonsailors tend to assume that a vessel's fastest point of sail is in the downwind direction because the vessel is traveling in the same direction as the wind. Under normal conditions, this is not so! The fastest point of sail for most vessels is when the wind is from the side (a reach), all sails are trimmed for maximum lift (the force providing the propulsion component) and a minimum drag (the force providing a reverse propulsion component). Sailing against the wind (pointing) also requires that the sails be trimmed for lift, but because of a less favorable apparent wind direction, the net propulsion force is usually reduced.

POINTING WITH THE SQUARE SAIL

The square sail is not ideally suited for pointing because the yard that supports the sail cannot be rotated close to the vessel's fore-and-aft centerline; the forward movement of the yard is limited by the forestay and the backward movement by the leeward shrouds.[6] Also, the sail cannot be set flat because of its long, unsupported vertical edge that tends to curl back toward the sail, so a broader wind from farther astern is required to fill the sail.[7] The Vikings optimized windward performance by means of their beitass (which became the bowsprit) and the use of the bowline and bridle. Three- and even four-point bridles (fig. 72) were eventually used to distribute the force to several points and minimize the curl of the luff.

The bowsprit method of improving the shape of the square sail was first implemented on European cogs and continued to all square-rigged ships because it eventually permitted sailing to within 6 points (67.5 degrees) of the wind.[8] Later some vessels were equipped with *bumpkins* (or bumkins), a short spar projecting forward on each side of the bow, to provide additional lead points for bowlines. When close hauled and utilizing bowlines and bridles for maximum pointing, the ship was said to sail on a bowline or stand on a taut bowline.[9] When fore-and-aft jibs and staysails were installed on square-rigged ships in the eighteenth century, the bowline-bridle arrangement lost its popularity because of the interference of the bowlines with the halyards and sheets required for hoisting and trimming the jibs and staysails.[10] Some clipper ship sail plans from the nineteenth century, however, show the use of bridles and bowlines (fig. 73).[11] As the clipper ship's goal was a fast passage, which could require maximum pointing, the crew could tolerate the interference of the bowlines with the sheets and halyards.

The bowline and bridle arrangement was used only on the lower square sails; it was not required on upper sails because at this elevation the apparent wind is from further aft (fig. 74). The air flowing close to the water is slowed down due to the friction between the air and the water; thus, the air closest to the water moves more slowly than the air higher up. Studies have been conducted that

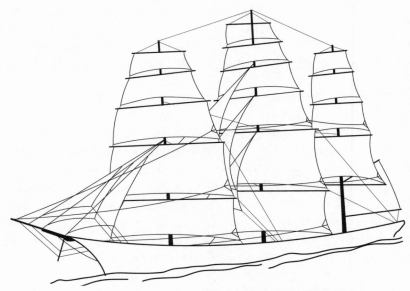

Figure 73. A clipper ship equipped with bowlines and bridles.

indicate if the wind speed is 5.4 knots at five feet above the water, the wind speed increases to 8.7 knots at fifty feet above the water (an increase of 60 percent).[12] This increase in wind speed at high levels results in a change in direction of the apparent wind (fig. 75); it blows from further aft and bowlines and bridles are not required to prevent the curl of the luff of the upper sails.

POINTING WITH FORE-AND-AFT SAILS

Because fore-and-aft sails can be trimmed close to the fore-and-aft centerline of the vessel, they can readily be trimmed for lift, even when the wind is substantially forward of the beam, which makes them ideally suited for high pointing. Also, the luff remains rigid due to its attachment to a mast or stay. (To review how the Dutch developed the fore-and-aft sail from the lateen, and how subsequent improvements allowed fore-and-aft rigged vessels to sail to about 45 degrees of the true wind and racing yachts to attain 32 to 39 degrees, see chapter 6.)[13] After about 1720, square-riggers were equipped with fore-and-aft jibs over the bowsprit, staysails forward of each mast, and a fore-and-aft spanker instead of a lateen steering sail. Some of these vessels had enough fore-and-aft-sail area to permit furling all square sails to become entirely fore-

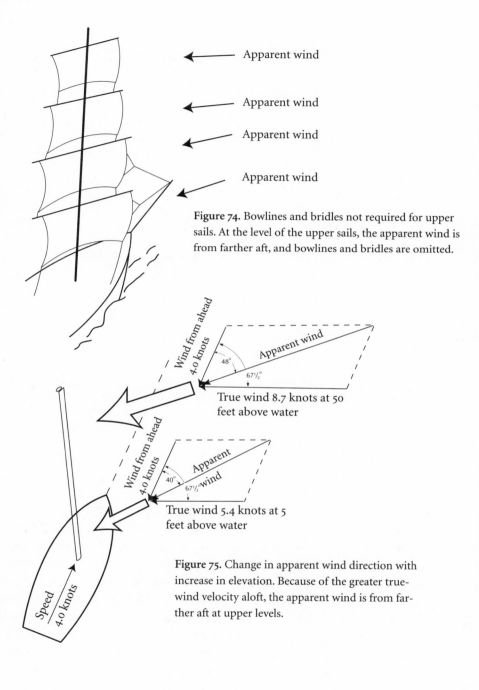

Apparent wind

Apparent wind

Apparent wind

Apparent wind

Figure 74. Bowlines and bridles not required for upper sails. At the level of the upper sails, the apparent wind is from farther aft, and bowlines and bridles are omitted.

Wind from ahead 4.0 knots

48°

Apparent wind

67½°

True wind 8.7 knots at 50 feet above water

Wind from ahead 4.0 knots

40°

Apparent wind

67½°

True wind 5.4 knots at 5 feet above water

Speed 4.0 knots

Figure 75. Change in apparent wind direction with increase in elevation. Because of the greater true-wind velocity aloft, the apparent wind is from farther aft at upper levels.

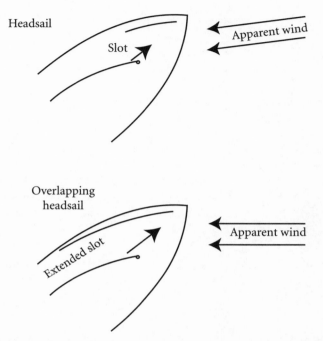

Figure 76. The slot effect. The greater low-pressure area provided by the extended slot and the greater sail area of the overlapping headsail provide a greater propulsion force.

and-aft rigged and in gale winds sailed fast and much more weatherly.[14]

THE SLOT EFFECT

On today's fore-and-aft rigged vessels, the headsail-mainsail arrangement forms a *venture-effect* funnel, a slot that increases the velocity and consequently lowers the pressure of the air flowing over the leeward (downwind) side of the mainsail. This is an example of Bernoulli's theorem stating that "when a flowing stream of gas speeds up, its pressure decreases," and it is the same effect that gives lift to the wings of aircraft. On a fore-and-aft-rigged vessel, it results in a great pressure difference across the mainsail and a greater propulsion force. If the headsail overlaps the mainsail to provide an extended slot, the greater pressure difference extends over a larger area of the sail and further improves mainsail's the performance (fig. 76). On today's racing and on some cruising sailboats, the extended slot effect is attained by means of the genoa (overlapping) jib. But the

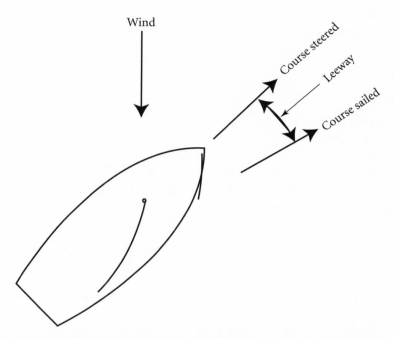

Wind

Course steered

Leeway

Course sailed

Figure 77. Leeway when sailing to windward. When plotting a course to windward, it is necessary to estimate leeway.

overlapping-sail concept was developed much earlier on American schooners.

LEEWAY

Except when the wind is from astern, a sailing vessel tends to slide along the surface of the water in the downwind direction. This downwind movement is called leeway (or making leeway) and detracts from the vessel's ability to sail to windward. The course actually sailed is further from the direction of the true wind than the course steered (fig. 77). Leeway can be minimized by increasing the lateral resistance of the hull.

PINCHING

Usually, the closer a vessel is sailed to the wind, the greater the leeway. Pinching is sailing as close to the wind as possible and is usually not justified because it results in maximum leeway and a loss of speed; however, the shape of the hull is a major factor in the magnitude of leeway. Pinching can also result in the lack of steering control until the vessel becomes completely unmanaged due to loss of forward movement. The practical approach in sailing close-hauled is to point as high as possible and yet maintain good speed.

Authorities on square-rig sailing disagree as to the maximum pointing capability of square-rigged vessels. According to Howard I. Chapelle, "A square-rig usually will not point much better than 5.5 points."[15] In contrast, Capt. Allan Villiers, one of the last square-rigger captains and a well known author says, "Six compass points from the wind. This was about as close to the wind as the usual square-rigger could hope to sail."[16] Probably Chapelle's 5.5 points (61.9 degrees) is the ultimate pointing in ideal wind and sea conditions and involves pinching, but Villiers's 6 points (67.5 degrees) is a more practical limit for general wind and sea conditions.

HEELING

Except when sailing downwind, a sailing vessel heels (leans) to leeward, particularly when sailing across the wind. This is not a permanent leaning, as with a list or roll due to wave action, but is caused by the wind striking the sail. If a vessel is not carrying a cargo of sufficient weight, ballast is required to pro-

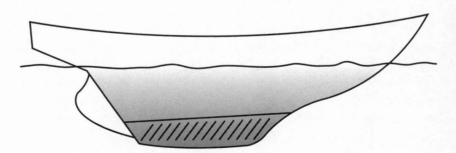

Figure 78. The ballast keel. The lead or cast iron within the keel is located as low as possible.

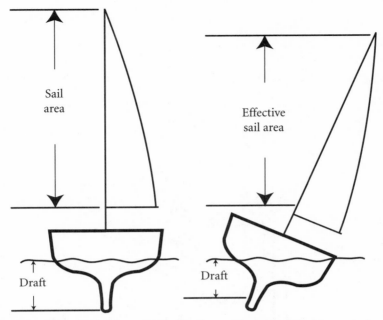

Figure 79. Excessive heel reduces draft and sail area. The reduced draft increases leeway, and the reduced effective sail area reduces propulsion force.

vide stability and avoid an excessive angle of heel. Rock and gravel were used as ballast in the days of sail, but in today's sailing yachts the ballast, usually lead or cast iron, is built into the keel (fig. 78).

Excessive heel is undesirable: it affects pointing and reduces speed. A high angle of heel increases leeway as the effective keel depth is reduced (fig. 79) and a larger bow wave is created on the leeward side than on the windward side. This larger bow wave forces the bow to windward and rudder action is required to prevent the vessel from turning into the wind (rounding up). Turning the rudder, in addition to changing the vessel's course, creates a brake effect that slows down the vessel.

Also, excessive heeling may nullify the ability of the rudder to steer the vessel. When the vessel is completely upright, the blade area of the rudder is in a vertical position, and the entire area acts to change the vessel's direction. With the slight angle of heel the rudder blade area is still effective in turning the vessel. At an excessive angle of heel, however, the blade area attains a vertical as well as a horizontal orientation and tends to act as an elevator as well

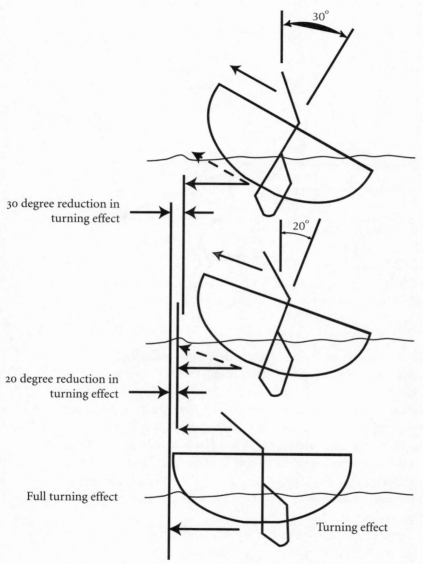

30°

30 degree reduction in
turning effect

20°

20 degree reduction in
turning effect

Full turning effect

Turning effect

Figure 80. Heeling reduces the turning effect of the rudder. The reduction in effectiveness can prevent the vessel from answering her helm.

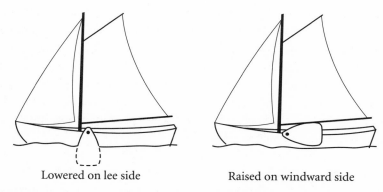

Lowered on lee side   Raised on windward side

Figure 81. Leeboards—a retractable keel. The leeboard minimizes leeway, but when the leeboard is raised it permits operating in shallow water and beaching the vessel.

as a rudder (fig. 80); the turning effect is drastically reduced and in a sudden gust of wind may not be sufficient to overcome the vessel's sudden tendency to turn into the wind (round-up). Loss of rudder control due to excessive heeling has resulted in collisions during sailboat races. When a port-tack racing sailboat is sailing hard on the wind and is on a collision course with a starboard-tack sailboat, the port-tack boat is required to tack or turn downwind. The starboard-tack boat is the stand-on boat (privileged) and is required to maintain course and speed. If the port-tack boat (with the burden to give way) elects to turn downwind and is prevented from doing so due to a sudden gust of wind that causes excessive heel, a collision is probable.

THE EFFECT OF THE KEEL AND THE DEVELOPMENT OF CENTERBOARDS

The keel is the lowest and strongest fore-and-aft centerline structural member of the hull, and on sailing vessels the keel is usually extended below the hull. The size, shape, and weight of the keel have a marked effect on a sailing vessel's performance and particularly on pointing. It was probably the development of the keel by the Phoenicians that allowed them to minimize leeway and sail against the wind and eventually to build ships without rowing ports.[17]

The keel, however, did not permit a vessel to operate in shallow water or to beach the vessel. To overcome these restrictions, the Dutch, in the first half of the fifteenth century, developed a retractable keel arrangement now known as a *leeboard*.[18] A leeboard was a flat wooden plate attached to the hull on either side of the vessel by means of a pivot on its upper end (fig. 81). When sailing against or across the wind, the board on the leeward side was placed in its low position to increase lateral resistance and minimize leeway. The windward board was pivoted into its upward position to eliminate frictional drag with the water. When sailing downwind, both boards were placed into the upward position; additional lateral resistance is not desirable when sailing directly downwind. The boards-up position also permitted beaching the vessel and operation in shallow water.

Leeboards are in common use today on sailing dinghies as are centerboards and daggerboards, which are located on the vessel centerline but perform the same function as leeboards (figs. 82 and 83). Although the colonial Americans are credited with the development of the pivotal centerboard to improve the windward performance of small, shallow-draft vessels, the concept of a retractable keel originated earlier. Some Chinese river junks were equipped with a sliding keel that could be raised or lowered within a watertight casing. In 1774, the British had a small vessel built in Boston with one long centerboard; later a larger vessel was built with three centerboards. In 1790 the British built a sixty-eight-foot revenue cutter with three centerboards, and in 1798 they launched a six-ton three-centerboard brig, the *Lady Nelson,* for a survey and discovery voyage around New South Wales. She was the first vessel to sail around Tasmania to discover that it was an island. The success of the *Lady Nelson* resulted in the construction of centerboard merchantmen to permit operation in very shallow waters.

In the United States work boats such as scows, skipjacks, bugeyes, catboats, oyster sloops, as well as many yachts are equipped with a pivoted centerboard. In addition to allowing shallow water operation, a centerboard vessel has an advantage over the full-keel vessel when sailing in a general downwind direction; the centerboard can be raised to reduce the wetted-surface friction, which increases speed.[19]

THE FRENCH CHASSE-MARÉE LUGGER

Prior to the introduction of cotton sailcloth and wire rope, probably the highest pointing sailing vessels were the French luggers of the chasse-marée type. These were fishing vessels initially, but later in the seventeenth and eighteenth centuries they were refined to serve as privateers and smugglers when speed and close windedness were primary requirements. These luggers had an extremely large sail area (making them tremendously overcanvased), three masts, a large bowsprit, and a long bumpkin (the spar extending over the stern). The total length of the bowsprit and bumpkin was almost equal to the length of the hull. The mainmast was located amidships, the foremast was well forward, and the mizzen was next to the stern transom, the aftermost side-to-side planking of the stern. The sails were the standing lug type with topsails, and a large jib was located over the long bowsprit (fig. 84). For maximum pointing, bowlines were attached to the luff of the mainsail and led to the foremast. A *foule* (spar) was inserted into the luff of the foresail in the same manner as the Vikings used their beitass. These two rigging arrangements, which had been developed by the Vikings for the square sail, were used to improve pointing of this fore-and-aft rig.

The chasse-marée luggers, however, had a disadvantage: they required a large crew. On the standing-lug rig, the sail and the lug remain on the same side of the mast when tacking; but for best performance all of the sails had to be on the leeward side because this provides the optimum sail shape. When tacking, this required *dipping* sails and lug. The sail had to be lowered, the lug moved to the opposite side of the mast, and then the lug and sail rehoisted. For maximum weatherability these standing-lug vessels had to be sailed as dipping lugs.[20] Another disadvantage was that when running before the wind, standing-lug vessels could usually be overtaken by a ship with a normal square rig.[21]

To windward these French luggers were faster and more weatherly than the English cutters. Off the wind, the cutters were faster because they carried large square topsails, but when linen sailcloth was replaced with cotton, and wire rope became available, the cutters outperformed the French luggers. The

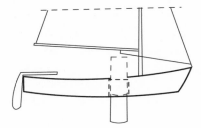

Figure 82. Centerboard.   **Figure 83.** Daggerboard.

The retractable keels are commonly used on trailable boats.

Figure 84. The French chasse-marée lugger. Because of their tremendous sail area, these eighteenth-century vessels were the fastest sailing vessels going to windward.

English cutter was the forerunner of the early racing yachts; luggers were not used for racing because of the difficulty in dipping the lug when tacking.[22]

FLAX VERSUS COTTON SAILCLOTH

Pliable flax, woven on foot-operated spinning wheels was used for sailcloth well into the eighteenth century. It remained soft and pliable when wet, an advantage for handling sails in bad weather; but with extended usage, the flax canvas stretched, sagged, and became porous. This resulted in a good sail shape for sailing downwind but bad for sailing to weather; a flat sail shape is best for sailing to windward.

In the early part of the nineteenth century, cotton was mixed with flax, and later, all-cotton canvas became available, which improved sailing upwind because it was more closely woven on power looms. Privateers and blockade runners with sails made of the new cloth were closer winded than the sailing vessels that used the old flax sails. Today, cotton cloth is inferior to synthetic-fiber sailcloth.[23]

Sails in China

and the

Pacific Islands

The foregoing has been a review of the evolutionary development of sails in Western civilization. Although there is a scarcity of documentation regarding the development of sailing technology in other areas, there is evidence of the early existence of high-performance sails in China and the islands of the Pacific.

CHINA

The European mariners that voyaged to the Far East referred to the Chinese as "Dutchmen of the East" because of their many significant nautical developments.[1] Their most famous maritime contribution is the magnetic compass. They also began using the stern-mounted rudder long before the Europeans, perhaps as early as the fourth century B.C.,[2] and even experimented with manual-powered sidewheel propulsion.[3] This propulsion system was the same system that was used on the first steam-powered vessels in the early 1800s.

The word *junk* comes from the Portuguese *junco*, which was adapted from the Javanese *djong*, meaning ship or large vessel.[4] Our earliest description of the Chinese junk is by Marco Polo in 1298.[5] He described large vessels that required a crew of up to three hundred and that voyaged from

Figure 85. The Chinese junk with retractable rudder, leeboards, and lazy jacks. Because of the many sail adjustments, exceptional competence was required to trim a junk's sails for optimum performance.

Kamchatka to Zanzibar and to the islands of the South Pacific.[6] There is some evidence that Chinese seafarers visited the coast of California before the time of Christ.[7] Between 1405 and 1433 Zheng Ho, a Chinese diplomat and naval leader, conducted seven major nautical expeditions to foreign lands in ships that were substantially larger than the European ships of that day. They carried huge cargoes and many soldiers. The ships sailed from Shanghai twenty-six hundred miles south to Java, then through the Malacca Strait to Ceylon (today's Sri Lanka), north to India, and to the Persian Gulf. Some of the voyagers continued to the Red Sea city of Mecca, and then south to Mogadishu and Malindi, the major Arab trade centers in East Africa. From these voyages the Chinese resolved that there was nothing of significant value in these foreign cultures; Chinese goods and practices were superior to that of the foreigners, and in 1433 overseas travel was forbidden to all Chinese.[8]

The Chinese junk was a sophisticated vessel (fig. 85). It had a flat bottom and a sloping bow to permit beaching and a stern mounted rudder that could be raised for beaching or lowered to act as a keel. The Chinese had developed leeboards long before the Dutch, to compensate for the lack of a true keel. Transverse bulkheads were used to limit flooding; this concept of compartmentation was not incorporated into European-built ships until the nineteenth century.[9] The transverse bulkheads allowed liquid cargoes: junks were the first tankers, and eighteenth-century junks were capable of shipping fifty tons of liquid cargo.[10] A high freeboard aft provided a greater sail area than a lower freeboard forward, allowing the junk to lie head to the wind in a gale, even with all sails doused.

Most junks were three masted. The sail on the foremast acted as a jib. The mainmast was located slightly forward of center and supported the largest sail. The mizzenmast was well aft and supported a sail that probably functioned as a steering sail. Some junks had two mizzen sails located on two masts, one on each quarter.[11]

The characteristic sail of the junk is a standing lug (the sail remains on the same side of the mast when tacking) and is somewhat similar in appearance to the settee sail of the Arab dhow (fig. 18). Each sail had several full-length horizontal battens (a light spar inserted into the sail) and sheets were attached to the after end of the battens. The lower sheets were led to deck level and the upper sheets to a mast astern or to the deck. This arrangement permitted the aerodynamic optimum sail adjustment for sailing to windward.[12] Because of the excessive weight of this arrangement and the shallow draft, however, the junk would not perform as well to windward as the typical fore-and-aft-rigged vessel.[13] The multiple full-length battens also simplified reefing, permitted rapid dousing of the sail, reinforced the sailcloth (a woven mat), and allowed the sail to lie flat (desirable for sailing to windward).

Lazy jacks were used in conjunction with the full-length battens to facilitate reefing and lowering the sail completely. The lazy jacks consisted of a system of ropes that formed a sling type of arrangement about the lower portion of the sail and the boom. When the sail was lowered, the lower portion was captured by the sling arrangement to prevent the wind from blowing it away from the boom. This Chinese invention of full-length battens and lazy jacks is frequently used on today's cruising yachts to aid in reefing and completely furling the mainsail (fig. 86).

It is generally believed that the Chinese initially obtained their knowledge of sailing from Indonesia.[14] The exact date and shape of their original sail has

Figure 86. Features inherited from the Chinese junk. Lazy jacks and full battens on a modern sailing yacht.

not been established; however, the junk sail was in use as early as the third century B.C.[15] and the Chinese were sailing upwind before the time of Christ. Long before the European Age of Discovery, the Chinese built larger and more seaworthy ships than did the Europeans and had more seagoing experience than the rest of the world put together.[16]

Surprisingly, the Chinese junk design penetrated into California in the mid-1800s. After the discovery of gold in California in 1848, many Chinese migrated to California to escape the flood, famine, war, and rebellion that followed the Opium Wars of 1839–1842 and 1856–1860, and the Taiping Rebellion of 1851–1864, a Chinese peasant uprising. The Chinese worked in mining and in the construction of the western half of the transcontinental railroad. Others entered their homeland occupations of agriculture and fishing.

The Chinese fishermen built and operated fishing vessels along the coast of California, but most were concentrated in San Diego Bay because this location permitted fishing the Baja Coast of Mexico as far south as Cape San Lucas. Most of their vessels were built in San Diego Bay. The smallest were single-masted sampans with a junk type of sail. The larger vessels were mostly two-masted junks, but at least one was a fifty-two-foot three-masted junk. By 1888 there were eighteen junks operating out of San Diego Bay. But their domination of the San Diego fishing industry was suddenly terminated by the 1892 Geary Act that prohibited the Chinese fishermen from reentering the country if their vessels passed outside the three-mile territorial limit.[17]

POLYNESIA

The Polynesians were outstanding sailors and navigators. Without compass or charts, they sailed their catamarans from New Zealand to Hawaii and possibly as far as South America.[18] Some anthropologists and archaeologists have called the Polynesians' voyages one of the greatest achievements of the human species—spanning the entire Pacific Ocean in four millennia.[19]

Without a written language they developed a system of navigation that has been referred to as *wayfinding*. It is based on knowledge of the movement of the sun and the stars; of wind and wave patterns; of the color of the sky; and of types of birds and fish with particular attributes. Polynesian sailors committed to memory all of these natural phenomena passed down from generation to generation.[20] In 1784 Capt. James Cook described their system of navigation: "The sun is their guide by day and the stars at night. When these are obscured, they have recourse to the points from which the waves and winds come upon the vessel. If during the observation the wind and waves should shift—they are then bewildered, frequently miss their intended port and are never heard of more."[21]

There are two schools of thought on the origins of Polynesian culture. Some believe that in about 1400 B.C. Indians from the American Pacific Northwest sailed twin-hulled dugout canoes to the islands of Polynesia, where they joined with earlier settlers from Peru.[22] The prevailing theory, however, is that possibly as early as 2000 B.C., the Polynesians migrated from Southeast Asia, through Indonesia, to settle in the Pacific Islands.[23] Indonesia consists of over thirteen thousand islands, an ideal location for the development of sails and the training of sailors. Here they probably developed their knowledge of oceanic seafaring,[24] which they took with them when they settled the islands of Oceania (the islands of the Pacific, including Melanesia, Micronesia, and Polynesia).

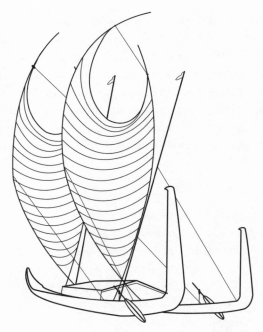

Figure 87. The Polynesian twin spritsail/crab claw sail. By spreading the sprits, the sail could be flattened for sailing to windward.

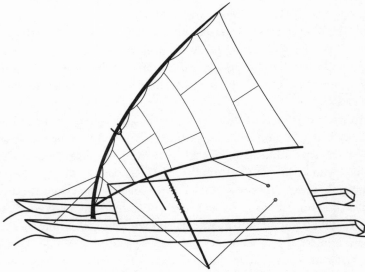

Figure 88. The Polynesian single spritsail. Reducing the bend of the sprit would flatten the sail for better windward performance.

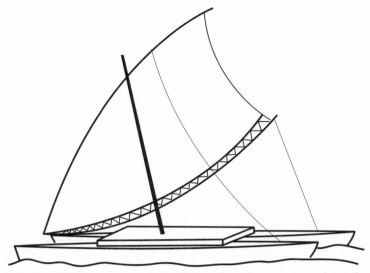

Figure 89. The Polynesian lateen sail. This triangular sail was surprisingly similar to the Mediterranean lateen.

The Polynesian sailing craft were equipped with a variety of sails that are generally categorized as oceanic spritsails. Originally the sail was suspended between two vertical masts, but later it evolved into a roughly triangular shape supported by two flexible masts or sprits. This sail was known as the twin spritsail and also as the *crab claw* sail (fig. 87).[25] Another arrangement was a sail attached to a single mast with a rigid bottom section and a flexible upper section. The flexible upper section of the mast (the sprit) permitted flattening the sail for sailing to windward (fig. 88). The Polynesian lateen sail (fig. 89) was remarkably similar in appearance to the Mediterranean lateen.

The Polynesian catamarans and outrigger canoes were capable of sailing upwind, and some historians have speculated that at least one version of the Oceanic spritsail crossed the Pacific: the Spanish explorer and conquistador Pizarro observed sailing rafts with sails of this type on the west coast of South America.[26] Recently a historically accurate model of a Polynesian sailing craft was tested to determine its performance in sailing to windward. The test revealed that the Polynesian sailing craft, at least of the type tested, could sail within about 60 degrees of the wind.[27]

The Minoan-Phoenician method of minimizing heeling under sail was to place sand or stones as ballast at the lowest level inside the hull. The Polynesian

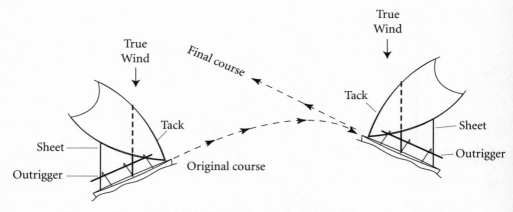

Figure 90. Reverse tacking the Polynesian outrigger canoe. The outrigger remains on the windward side before and after tacking.

concept used two hulls separated a convenient distance apart and attached by rigid members. Today this twin-hull arrangement is known as a catamaran. Buddy Ebsen, the actor of movie and television fame, built a twin-hulled sailing yacht and named it *Polynesian Concept*. In 1968, his *Polynesian Concept* won the Third Biennial Multihull Transpacific Yacht Race from San Pedro, California, to Honolulu.[28]

The Polynesian twin-hulled canoes could be tacked in the conventional manner, but conventional tacking was not feasible for the single-hull outrigger canoes because the outrigger always had to remain on the windward side (fig. 90). The outrigger balanced the canoe with its weight, not its buoyancy. If the outrigger were positioned on the leeward side, a sudden gust of wind could submerge it, causing a sudden turn in the downwind direction and possibly breaking off the outrigger. To prevent such a disaster, the Polynesians developed an ingenious method of reversing the bow and stern during the tack so that the outrigger always remained on the windward side.

The mast of these outrigger sailing canoes was stepped in the center of the canoe and was tipped forward. The single sail had a bowed V shape and each leg of the V was attached to a light spar similar to the Polynesian lateen shown in figure 89. Prior to tacking, it was first necessary to reduce forward movement by pointing the bow into the wind (luffing-up to reduce headway) and

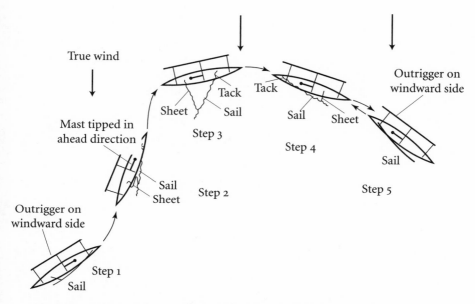

Figure 91. Step-by-step procedure for tacking the Polynesian outrigger canoe.

1. Underway on original course.
2. Luff-up to reduce headway. Cast sheet loose.
3. Fall-off until wind is abeam. Slope mast toward stern. Sheet is still loose; sail is flapping to leeward.
4. Shift tack to the new bow and the sheet to the new stern.
5. Tighten sheet. Underway on new course.

then placing the vessel broadside to the wind. The sheet was then slacked to allow the sail to flap to leeward. The tack of the sail was then moved to the new bow and the mast was tilted toward the new forward direction. The sheet was then led to the new stern position and tightened to allow the sail to propel the vessel in the new ahead direction (fig. 91).[29]

Another type of canoe was the double outrigger, but it existed only in Indonesia; there is no evidence of a double-outrigger canoe ever having been seen in the Polynesian islands. There was also the single hull without outrigger,

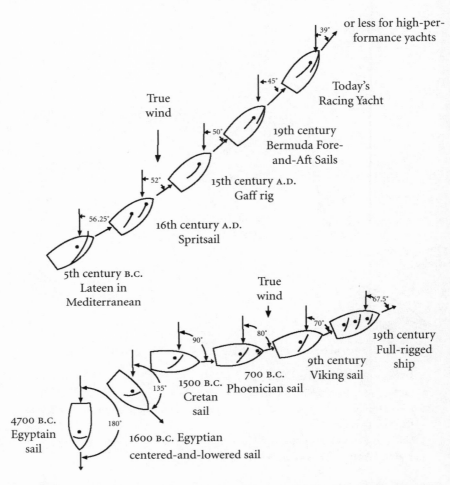

Figure 92. The performance of sails through the centuries. Gradually through the centuries humans learned to sail: first downwind, then across the wind, and finally against the wind.

which the Maoris used as war canoes. They existed only in New Zealand where tree trunks were large enough to make them, and they were propelled only by paddles.[30]

It is interesting to note that explorers from the Western world conducted their explorations with sailing vessels that were less efficient sailing to windward than the sailing craft of the Polynesians.[31] It is also of interest to perceive that the Polynesians were probably sailing to windward when sailors of the Western civilization were only just experimenting with sailing across the wind.

THE VITALITY OF SAILING

Today, ocean and inland waterway commerce is by diesel-powered vessels. Warships are propelled by steam and by gas turbines. Sailing is now a sport for recreational and racing sailors. It appears that the Great Age of Sail that began in the fourteenth century is now over. Not so! Among others, the fore-and-aft sails and square sails, whose development through the centuries is traced in figure 92, are still very much in use. The United States Coast Guard trains their future officers aboard the *Eagle,* a seagoing three-masted bark. Brazil has a true clipper ship; Indonesia has a barkentine; and Uruguay has a three-masted bark. There are now about fifty oceangoing sail training-ships, and these ships are now classified as *tall ships* to differentiate them from cruising and racing yachts.

Tall ships are also operated by museums and even cities: examples include the *Priscilla,* an 1888 schooner restored by the Long Island Maritime Museum; the *Elissa* from Galveston (the Tall Ships for Texas); and the *Star of India,* in San Diego Bay, the oldest active sailing vessel in the world. Also, in the last few years, replicas of historic ships have been built, such as Captain Cook's *Endeavour* and the *Californian,* a replica of the nineteenth-century revenue cutter.

For the 1964 World's Fair, New York hosted the first Operation Sail, and seven tall ships participated. At that time it was believed that this would be the last opportunity to get these tall ships together. But the popularity of the event resulted in additional OP Sails held in New York: for America's bicentennial observation in 1976; for the hundredth birthday of the Statue of Liberty in 1986; and for the quincentennial celebration in 1992 commemorating Columbus's arrival in the New World. These parades of tall ships have enthralled thousands of landlubbers and mariners alike. "More people have gathered for past OP Sails than for any other purpose, ever, in America."[32]

Operation Sail 2000 was among the grandest events. The tall ships from all over the world gathered in San Juan, Puerto Rico, in March 2000, and spent the summer parading through the East Coast port cities of Miami, Norfolk, Baltimore, and Philadelphia. On 4 July 2000, 182 tall ships paraded on the

Hudson to celebrate the nation's birthday and to fulfill Operation Sail's stated mission that "every person in America should understand the importance of the ship, the ocean, and the waterways in our nation's history." As long as our nation's landlubbers and mariners maintain this enthusiasm for the glory of the sail, the Age of Sail will endure.

Notes

References to books are shortened in the notes but fully cited in the bibliography. First use of other sources, such as articles, encyclopedias, and museums are fully cited in the notes. These sources do not appear in the bibliography.

CHAPTER 1. EGYPT AND THE EARLY MEDITERRANEAN

1. Johnstone, *The Sea Craft of Prehistory*, 75, 211.
2. Mansir, *Modeler's Guide*, 9.
3. Tunis, *Oars, Sails, and Steam*, 14.
4. Johnstone, *Sea Craft of Prehistory*, 75–77.
5. Mansir, *Art of Ship Modeling*, 48.
6. Tunis, *Oars, Sails, and Steam*, 15.
7. Phillips-Birt, *History of Seamanship*, 36.
8. Ibid., 40–43.
9. Ibid., 37–38.
10. Casson, *Ancient Mariners*, 9–13.
11. Phillips-Birt, *History of Seamanship*, 39–45.
12. Anderson and Anderson, *Sailing Ship*, 24.
13. *The World Book Encyclopedia*, 2001 ed., Salamis.
14. Casson, *Ancient Mariners*, 20.
15. Mansir, *Art of Ship Modeling*, 50.
16. Anderson and Anderson, *Sailing Ship*, 29.
17. Maloney, *Chapman*, 188.
18. Mansir, *Modeler's Guide*, 16.
19. Kent, *History of Ships*, 23.
20. Ibid., 36.
21. Mansir, *Art of Ship Modeling*, 51.

22. Kent, *History of Ships*, 18–21.
23. Casson, *Ships and Seamanship*, 66.
24. Kent, *History of Ships*, 18–21.
25. Casson, *Ships and Seamanship*, 70.
26. Kent, *History of Ships*, 18–21.
27. *World Book*, 2001 ed., Phoenicia.
28. Chatterton, *Sailing Ships*, 10.
29. Casson, *Ancient Mariners*, 159–66.
30. *Encyclopedia Americana*, International ed., Punic Wars.
31. Mahan, preface to *Influence of Sea Power*, iv–v; see also introduction, 10–12.
32. Kemp, ed., *Oxford Companion to Ships*, 536.
33. Mansir, *Modeler's Guide*, 18.
34. Anderson and Anderson, *Sailing Ship*, 49.
35. Casson, *Illustrated History*, 56.
36. Mansir, *Modeler's Guide*, 59.

CHAPTER 2. THE LATEEN SAIL

1. Chatterton, *Sailing Ships*, 45.
2. Anderson and Anderson, *Sailing Ship*, 102–3.
3. Ibid.
4. Harland, *Seamanship in the Age of Sail*, 60.
5. Casson, *Illustrated History*, 163.
6. Casson, *Ships and Seamanship*, 268.
7. Anderson and Anderson, *Sailing Ship*, 103.
8. Casson, *Ships and Seamanship*, 244.
9. Chatterton, *Sailing Ships*, 43.
10. Casson, *Ships and Seamanship*, 277.
11. Mansir, *Modeler's Guide*, 31.
12. Villiers, *Monsoon Seas*, 54–57.
13. Ibid., 6–7.
14. Kemp, *History of Ships*, 52.
15. Casson, *Illustrated History*, 181.
16. Villiers, *Monsoon Seas*, 75.

CHAPTER 3. THE VIKING CONTRIBUTION

1. Mansir, *Modeler's Guide*, 22.
2. Casson, *Illustrated History*, 59.
3. Chatterton, *Sailing Ships*, 90–91.

4   Mansir, *Art of Ship Modeling,* 63.

5. Johnstone, *Sea Craft of Prehistory,* 117.

6. Kemp, *History of Ships,* 45.

7. *World Book,* 2001 ed., Vikings.

8. Ibid.

9. Phillips-Birt, *History of Seamanship,* 113.

10. Atkinson, *Viking Ships,* 11–12.

11. Woodman, *History of the Ship,* 28.

12. Mansir, *Art of Ship Modeling,* 61.

13. Angeluci and Cucari, *Ships,* 42.

14. Casson, *Illustrated History,* 63.

15. Kemp, *History of Ships,* 59.

16. Ibid., 71.

17. Ibid., 59.

18. Anderson and Anderson, *Sailing Ship,* 88.

19. Kemp, ed., *Oxford Companion to Ships,* 373.

20. Ibid., 57.

CHAPTER 4. THE FULL-RIGGED SHIP

1. Casson, *Illustrated History,* 81.

2. Angeluci and Cucari, *Ships,* 38.

3. Mansir, *Modeler's Guide,* 54.

4. Casson, *Illustrated History,* 84.

5. Ibid., 82.

6. Mansir, *Modeler's Guide,* 42; Kemp, ed., *Oxford Companion to Ships,* 139.

7. For caravel redonda, see Kemp, *History of Ships,* 76; for carrack, see Tunis, *Oars, Sails, and Steam,* 25–27.

8. Kemp, ed., *Oxford Companion to Ships,* 572.

9. Villiers, *Monsoon Seas,* 118–21.

10. Bathe, Rubin De Cervin, and Taillemite, *Great Age of Sail,* 12.

11. Villiers, *Monsoon Seas,* 118–21.

12. Kemp, *History of Ships,* 81.

13. Kemp, ed., *Oxford Companion to Ships,* 246–47.

14. Ibid., 337.

15. Woodman, *History of the Ship,* 58–59.

16. Bathe, Rubin De Cervin, and Taillemite, *Great Age of Sail,* 12.

17. Reference to the first globe in Kemp, *History of Ships,* 73–74; reference to magnetic compass in Woodman, *History of the Ship,* 42.

18. Anderson and Anderson, *Sailing Ship,* 126–29.

19. Kemp, *History of Ships,* 70–74.
20. For galleon see Woodman, *History of the Ship,* 58–59; for carrack see Tunis, *Oars, Sails, and Steam,* 25–27.
21. Kemp, ed., *Oxford Companion to Ships,* 511.
22. Peter Stanford, "Sir Francis Drake Sails for Freedom," *Sea History,* National Maritime Historical Society (winter 1996–1997), 8–11.
23. Kemp, ed., *Oxford Companion to Ships,* 470–71.
24. Raymond Aker, "Reconstructing Drake's Golden Hind," *Mains'l Haul,* Mariners Museum of San Diego (fall 2000): 15–20.
25. Kirsch, *Galleon,* 8.
26. Kemp, ed., *Oxford Companion to Ships,* 516.
27. Stanford, "Drake Sails for Freedom," 8–11.
28. Casson, *Illustrated History,* 98.
29. Ibid.
30. Ibid.
31. Phillips-Birt, *History of Seamanship,* 204–5.
32. Ibid.
33. Ibid.
34. Bathe, Rubin De Cervin, and Taillemite, *Great Age of Sail,* 55–56.
35. Kemp, *The History of Ships,* 100.
36. Casson, *Illustrated History,* 102–3

CHAPTER 5. THE SQUARE RIG

1. Casson, *Ships and Seamanship,* 224–25.
2. Woodman, *History of the Ship,* 39.
3. Kemp, *History of Ships,* 59.
4. For steerage see Woodman, *History of the Ship,* 39; also Kemp, ed., *Oxford Companion to Ships,* 831.
5. Harland, *Seamanship in the Age of Sail,* 174.
6. Kemp, *History of Ships,* 121.
7. Chatterton, *Sailing Ships,* 245–51.
8. Woodman, *History of the Ship,* 71–86.
9. Tryckare, *Lore of Ships,* 98.
10. Casson, *Illustrated History,* 107–11.
11. Kemp, *History of Ships,* 110.
12. Kemp, ed., *Oxford Companion to Ships,* 152.
13. Kemp, *History of Ships,* 131.
14. Kemp, ed., *Oxford Companion to Ships,* 329.
15. Casson, *Illustrated History,* 162.
16. Kemp, ed., *Oxford Companion to Ships,* 95.

17. Ibid., 87.
18. Ibid., 625.

CHAPTER 6. THE FORE-AND-AFT RIG

 1. Chatterton, *Sailing Ships,* 282–83.
 2. Mansir, *Modeler's Guide,* 60.
 3. Casson, *Ships and Seamanship,* 243–44.
 4. Phillips-Birt, *History of Seamanship,* 223–25.
 5. Kemp, *History of Ships,* 122.
 6. Ross, with Chapman, *Sail Power,* 226.
 7. Mansir, *Modeler's Guide,* 60.
 8. Kemp, ed., *Oxford Companion to Ships,* 80.
 9. Casson, *Illustrated History,* 18.
10. Kemp, ed., *Oxford Companion to Ships,* 655.
11. Conner, *Comeback,* 87.
12. Kemp, ed., *Oxford Companion to Ships,* 364.
13. Casson, *Illustrated History,* 194–97.
14. Phillips-Birt, *History of Seamanship,* 264–65; see also Kemp, ed., *Oxford Companion to Ships,* 161.
15. Casson, *Illustrated History,* 171.
16. Ibid., 181.
17. Tryckare, *Lore of Ships,* 97.

CHAPTER 7. TWO CLASSIC SAILING RIGS

 1. Villiers, *Captain James Cook,* 294.
 2. Kemp, *History of Ships,* 197.
 3. Tryckare, *Lore of Ships,* 250.
 4. Lecture aboard the brig *Pilgrim,* operated by the Ocean Institute, Dana Point, Calif., 23 June 2001.
 5. Kemp, ed., *Oxford Companion to Ships,* 227.
 6. Ibid., 706.
 7. Ibid., 814.
 8. Ibid., 821.
 9. *Star of India* exhibit, Maritime Museum of San Diego, Calif.
10. Kemp, ed., *Oxford Companion to Ships,* 146.
11. Kerchov, *Marine Dictionary,* 328.
12. Woodman, *History of the Ship,* 92.
13. Ibid., 328.
14. Kemp, ed., *Oxford Companion to Ships,* 656, 946.

15. Villiers, *Captain James Cook*, 86–87.
16. Casson, *Illustrated History*, 102–3.
17. Chatterton, *Sailing Ships*, 305.
18. Casson, *Illustrated History*, 190–91.
19. Kemp, ed., *Oxford Companion to Ships*, 302, 847.
20. Bathe, Rubin De Cervin, and Taillemite, *Great Age of Sail*, 241.
21. *Balclutha* exhibit, San Francisco Historic Park, San Francisco, Calif.
22. *Prussen* exhibit, San Francisco Historic Park, San Francisco, Calif.; see also Bathe, Rubin De Cervin, and Taillemite, *Great Age of Sail*, 254–58.
23. Casson, *Illustrated History*, 159.
24. Peter Stanford, "The Cape Horn Road," part 21, *Sea History*, National Maritime Historical Society (winter 1999–2000): 10.
25. *Kenilworth* exhibit, San Francisco Historic Park, San Francisco, Calif.

CHAPTER 8. POINTS OF SAIL

1. Kemp, ed., *Oxford Companion to Ships*, 173, 331, 614, 656.
2. Chapelle, *Search for Speed under Sail*, 23–25.
3. Lecture aboard the brig *Pilgrim*, operated by the Ocean Institute, Dana Point, Calif., 23 June 2001.

CHAPTER 9. SAIL AREA ADJUSTMENTS

1. Casson, *Ships and Seamanship*, 38–39.
2. Ibid., 277.
3. Kemp, ed., *Oxford Companion to Ships*, 839.
4. Villiers, *Battle of Trafalgar*, 35, 36.
5. Ibid., 69.
6. Ibid., 24–33.
7. Ibid., 85.
8. Mahan, preface to *Influence of Sea Power*, iv.
9. Kemp, ed., *Oxford Companion to Ships*, 822.
10. Kerchov, *Marine Dictionary*, 769.
11. Tom Whidden, "A Rose by Any Name," *Yachting*, April 1996, 18.

CHAPTER 10. SCHOONERS

1. Kemp, ed., *Oxford Companion to Ships*, 759.
2. MacGregor, *Schooners in Four Centuries*, 16–19.
3. Ibid., 127.

4. Ibid., 34.

5. Gloucester schooner exhibit, Mystic Seaport Museum, Mystic, Conn.

6. MacGregor, *Schooners in Four Centuries,* 127.

7. Kemp, *History of Ships,* 211.

8. Kemp, ed., *Oxford Companion to Ships,* 55.

9. Ibid., 690.

10. MacGregor, *Schooners in Four Centuries,* 34.

11. Ibid., 74.

12. Ibid., 25–27.

13. Ibid.

14. Casson, *Illustrated History,* 142.

15. John Barnard, with William MacIntosh, "Baltimore, a Renaissance City," *Sea History,* National Maritime Historic Society (spring 1998), 30–32.

16. MacGregor, *Schooners in Four Centuries,* 74.

17. Ibid., 39–43.

18. Scow schooner exhibit, San Francisco Historic Park, San Francisco, Calif.

19. MacGregor, *Schooners in Four Centuries,* 52–62.

20. For "all hands" see Phillips-Birt, *History of Seamanship,* 273; for "one survivor" see Kemp, ed., *Oxford Companion to Ships,* 865.

21. MacGregor, *Schooners in Four Centuries,* 60–71.

22. Ibid., 58–60.

23. Kemp, ed., *Oxford Companion to Ships,* 18–19.

24. Conner and Levitt, *America's Cup,* 2.

25. Joshua Humphreys was the designer of the USS *Constitution, Constellation,* and other large frigates equipped with guns (cannons) that were larger than those carried by the typical frigates of that era and thus able to shoot larger and heavier balls.

CHAPTER 11. THE REIGN OF THE CLIPPER SHIP

1. Anderson and Anderson, *Sailing Ship,* 188.

2. Whipple, *Clipper Ships,* 23.

3. Ibid., 24–25.

4. Kemp, ed., *Oxford Companion to Ships,* 172.

5. Morison, *Maritime History of Massachusetts,* 349.

6. Silverberg, *Nat Palmer,* 106–30.

7. Ibid., 157.

8. Morison, *Maritime History of Massachusetts,* 329.

9. Maloney, *Chapman,* 18.

10. Kemp, ed., *Oxford Companion to Ships,* 829.

11. Whipple, *Clipper Ships*, 51.
12. Stein, *Story of the Clipper Ships*, 15.
13. See Whipple, *Clipper Ships*, 51.
14. Tunis, *Oars, Sails, and Steam*, 51.
15. Anderson and Anderson, *Sailing Ship*, 191.
16. Kemp, ed., *Oxford Companion to Ships*, 172.
17. Stein, *Story of the Clipper Ships*, 18.
18. Ibid.
19. Kemp, *History of Ships*, 198–201.
20. Kemp, ed., *Oxford Companion to Ships*, 37.
21. Tunis, *Oars, Sails, and Steam*, 51.
22. Anderson and Anderson, *Sailing Ship*, 192.
23. Kemp, ed., *Oxford Companion to Ships*, 172.
24. Bathe, Rubin De Cervin, and Taillemite, *Great Age of Sail*, 213.
25. Whipple, *Clipper Ships*, 142.
26. Bathe, Rubin De Cervin, and Taillemite, *Great Age of Sail*, 213.
27. Whipple, *Clipper Ships*, 142.
28. Stein, *Story of the Clipper Ships*, 10.
29. Ibid.
30. Kemp, ed., *Oxford Companion to Ships*, 534–35.
31. *Jane's American Fighting Ships of the Twentieth Century* (New York: Modern Publishing, 1995), 152.
32. Chatterton, *Sailing Ships*, 310.
33. Morison, preface to *Maritime History of Massachusetts*, n.p.
34. Down-easter exhibit, San Diego Maritime Museum, San Diego, Calif.
35. Casson, *Illustrated History*, 156.

CHAPTER 12. WEATHERLINESS

1. Phillips-Birt, *History of Seamanship*, 223–25.
2. Chapelle, *Search for Speed under Sail*, 23–25.
3. Phillips-Birt, *History of Seamanship*, 281.
4. Kemp, ed., *Oxford Companion to Ships*, 464.
5. Tom Whidden, "What Tall Tails Tell You," *Yachting*, January 1997, 28.
6. Harland, *Seamanship in the Age of Sail*, 62.
7. Tryckare, *Lore of Ships*, 245.
8. Villiers, *Captain James Cook*, 294.
9. Kemp, ed., *Oxford Companion to Ships*, 102.
10. Tryckare, *Lore of Ships*, 71.
11. Ibid., 121.

12. Tom Whidden, "Let's Twist Again," *Yachting*, February 1998, 28.

13. Conner, *Comeback*, 87.

14. Chapelle, *Search for Speed under Sail*, 23–25.

15. Ibid.

16. Villiers, *Captain James Cook*, 294.

17. Mansir, *Modeler's Guide*, 16.

18. Kemp, ed., *Oxford Companion to Ships*, 473.

19. Ibid., 148.

20. Phillips-Brit, *History of Seamanship*, 264–66.

21. Kemp, ed., *Oxford Companion to Ships*, 161.

22. Phillips-Brit, *History of Seamanship*, 266.

23. Ibid., 269.

CHAPTER 13. SAILS IN CHINA AND THE PACIFIC ISLANDS

1. Chatterton, *Sailing Ships*, 310–11.

2. Casson, *Illustrated History*, 176–77.

3. Johnstone, *Sea Craft of Prehistory*, 192.

4. Kemp, ed., *Oxford Companion to Ships*, 437; Kemp, *History of Ships*, 54.

5. Kemp, ed., *Oxford companion to Ships*, 131.

6. Johnstone, *Sea Craft of Prehistory*, 185.

7. Mansir, *Art of Ship Modeling*, 78–79.

8, Peter Stanford, "The Cape Horn Road," part 14, *Sea History*, National Maritime Society (spring 1998): 10–15.

9. Casson, *Illustrated History*, 176–77.

10. Woodman, *History of the Ship*, 38.

11. Casson, *Illustrated History*, 176–77.

12. Tunis, *Oars, Sails, and Steam*, 52.

13. Chatterton, *Sailing Ships*, 311–12.

14. Johnstone, *Sea Craft of Prehistory*, 192.

15. Casson, *Illustrated History*, 176–77.

16. Johnstone, *Sea Craft of Prehistory*, 192.

17. Murray K. Lee, "The Chinese Fishing Industry of San Diego," *Mains'l Haul*, Maritime Museum Association of San Diego (summer 1999): 6–13.

18. Johnstone, *Sea Craft of Prehistory*, 218.

19. Ibid., 192.

20. Paine, *Ships of the World*, 235.

21. As quoted in Phillips-Birt, *History of Seamanship*, 283.

22. Mansir, *Art of Ship Modeling*, 10–15.

23. Johnstone, *Sea Craft of Prehistory*, 24.

24. Dodd, *Polynesian Seafaring*, 20.
25. Casson, *Illustrated History*, 207.
26. Johnstone, *Sea Craft of Prehistory*, 225.
27. Dodd, *Polynesian Seafaring*, 57.
28. Ebsen, with Guston, *Polynesian Concept*, 26.
29. Dodd, *Polynesian Seafaring*, 138–39.
30. Ibid., 22.
31. Ibid., 57.
32. As quoted in Peter Stanford, "How the Tall Ships Sail Today for Our Tomorrows," *Sea History*, National Maritime Society (autumn 1997), 10–11.

Glossary

aback	A sail is said to be aback when the wind impinges on the sail to force the vessel astern.
abaft	Toward the stern.
abeam	A direction at right angles to the fore-and-aft line of the vessel.
abreast	The position of another vessel or object that is abeam.
adrift	Denotes floating at random.
aft	At or toward the stern.
alee	The position of the helm to turn the vessel into the wind in order to start a tack.
aloft	Higher than the upper deck; above.
amidships	The middle of the vessel.
apparent wind	The resultant (compromise) wind created by the true wind that is actually blowing and the wind created by the forward movement of the vessel.
astern	Behind a vessel; also to move a vessel backwards.
backstay	A mast support extending from a high point on the mast toward the stern at deck level.
bald-headed	A sailing vessel underway without her headsails set.
ballast	Weight carried in a vessel to provide stability.
ballast keel	A keel that usually includes lead or cast iron to provide stability.
batten	A lightweight wooden or plastic strip inserted into a pocket on the sail to improve the shape of the sail.
beam	The width of a vessel.
beam ends	A vessel is said to be on her beam ends when she is heeled to such an extent that her deck beams are nearly vertical.
beat	Sailing to windward by means of successive tacks.
belaying pin	A short length of wood or metal in a rack to which running rigging can be secured.
bilge keel	A longitudinal projection on each side of the bottom of the hull and parallel to the hull to minimize rolling.

binnacle	A housing for the compass.
block	A wooden or metal pulley.
bonaventure mast	The fourth mast on some carracks and galleons.
boom	A horizontal spar to which the foot of a fore-and-aft sail is attached.
bow	The forward end of a vessel.
braces	Ropes attached to the ends of the yards (on a square-rigged ship) to position the yards at different angles to the fore-and-aft line of the ship.
breeze, land and sea	A coastal wind that blows from the sea in daytime and from the land at night.
bridle	A length of rope or wire attached at both ends to a spar, sail, or other object.
Bristol fashion	Everything in excellent condition, neat and seamanlike.
broach-to	The tendency of a vessel to turn into the wind when sailing downwind.
bulkhead	A transverse partitions on a ship.
bulwark	The wood planking or steel plate along the sides of a ship above the upper deck to prevent seas from washing over the side and to prevent persons on board from falling overboard.
bumpkin (bumkin)	Originally on square-rigged ships, a short boom projecting forward on each side of the bow and/or extending from each quarter for trimming square sails. Later, bumpkin (or bumkin) became the name of the short spar that extended over the stern to attach the sheet of a fore-and-aft sail that also extended over the stern.
buntline	A rope used for hauling the foot of a square sail toward its yard to permit reefing or furling the sail.
by the stern	When a vessel is drawing more than her normal depth of water aft.
Cape Horner	Usually a full-rigged ship that made regular passages around Cape Horn.
capstan	A rotating drum used to hoist the anchor or used for other heavy lifting. Originally the drum was rotated manually, by means of capstan bars inserted into the capstan, but later the drum was rotated mechanically by steam or electricity.
cast of the lead	The act of heaving a lead line to ascertain the depth of water.
centerboard	A board that is raised or lowered to perform the function of a keel in its lowered position.
claw off	Beating to windward to avoid being driven downwind onto a lee shore.

clew or clue	The aftermost corner of a fore-and-aft sail.
close-hauled	A condition of sailing in which the sails are trimmed to permit sailing as close to the wind as possible.
crow's nest	A small shelter on the foremast for a lookout.
dagger board	A vertical sliding centerboard.
donkey engine	A small auxiliary steam engine with its own small boiler used for providing power for hoisting the anchor and for hoisting sails.
dory	A small flat-bottom boat with sloping sides that allows nesting one boat within another.
draft	The depth of water which a vessel draws.
drift	The distance a vessel makes to leeward while proceeding on her desired course.
fall off	A sailing vessel falls off when she alters her course to leeward.
fathom	Six feet.
fender	A resilient object let down between the side of a vessel and a wharf or other vessel to prevent damage to the hull.
foot	The bottom side of a sail.
footropes	Horizontal ropes, supported at intervals by vertical ropes attached to a yard, to support seamen when they are aloft to furl, reef, or unfurl a square sail.
fore-and-aft rig	An arrangement of sails that permits positioning the sails close to the vessel's fore-and-aft centerline.
forecastle	Pronounced *fo'c'sle;* a short raised deck at the forward end of a vessel.
foremast	The most forward mast (except on a ketch or yawl).
freeboard	The vertical part of the hull that extends from the waterline to the deck level (free of the water).
furl	The process of gathering in a sail and securing it with gaskets to a boom or yard.
gaff	A spar to which the head of a four-sided fore-and-aft sail is attached.
gale	A wind of a velocity between thirty-four and forty-seven knots.
gasket	A rope, cord, or strip of canvas used to secure a sail when furling it to a yard or boom.
genoa jib	A large jib with a clew that extends much further aft than an ordinary jib so that it overlaps the mainsail by an appreciable amount.
gooseneck	A metal fitting, on a fore-and-aft rig, used to attach the forward end of the boom to the mast permitting the boom to swing to port and starboard.

ground tackle	A general term for anchors, cables, and mooring lines that are carried aboard to permit a ship to anchor or moor.
harden-in	Hauling in the sheet(s) of a sailing vessel.
head	The top or forward part; the top corner of the sail; the top of the mast (masthead); the bow part of the ship; also the lavatory.
headsail	Any triangular sail set forward (ahead) of the most forward mast.
heave-to	To position a sailing vessel relative to the wind so that she makes no headway.
heaving line	A light line with a small weight at the end.
heel	The leaning of a vessel to one side due to the wind force on the sails.
helm	The tiller or wheel that controls the position of the rudder.
hull	The main body of a ship that is apart from masts, rigging, and above deck cabins.
in stays (in irons)	When a vessel is head to wind and cannot sail on either tack.
jib	A triangular sail ahead of the foremast.
jibe (gybe), to wear ship	Changing direction so that the stern passes through the direction from which the wind is blowing.
keel	The lowest and principal centerline structural member of the hull.
knock down	A sailing vessel that is rolled over so that her mast(s) and sails are in the water.
larboard	The old term for the left-hand side of the vessel when it is facing forward. In the early nineteenth century, the name was changed to *port*.
lash	To secure anything with a rope or cord.
lead line	A line to which a lead weight is attached to one end for measuring the depth of water.
lee	Downwind; the lee of leeward side of the ship is the downwind side.
leeboard	A drop keel on each side of a small sailing vessel. To minimize the vessel's drift to leeward, the board on the lee side is lowered.
leech	The side of a square sail; the after edge of a fore-and-aft sail.
leeway	The distance a sailing vessel is set down to leeward of her desired course.
leg	The distance sailed on a single tack.

list	An inclining of a vessel to one side or the other, usually due to a shift in the cargo or flooring of some part of the hull.
luff	The leading edge of a fore-and-aft sail.
mainmast	The second and tallest mast when there are two or more masts (except on ketches and yawls, where the forward mast is the mainmast).
mainsail	The principal sail of a sailing vessel. On a square-rigged vessel it is the lowermost and largest sail carried on the mainmast and is usually called the main course. On the fore-and-aft rig it is the sail carried on the mainmast.
mainsail haul	The order given on a square-rigged ship when tacking to position the mainsail for the next tack. The order is given after the sails on the foremast have been backed and the ship is nearly head to wind.
mast	A vertical spar. On a sailing vessel, a mast's primary purpose is to carry sails; on mechanically propelled vessels the mast serves to carry radar arrays, aerials, lights, and signal flags.
mizzen	The name of the third, usually the aftermost, mast of a sailing ship.
nautical mile	6,080 feet.
off the wind	Sailing with the wind from abaft the beam.
on the wind	Sailing as close to the wind as possible.
painter	A short length of rope used to secure a boat to a pier, jetty, or ship.
peak	The upper after corner of a four-sided fore-and-aft sail.
pendant	A length of rope or wire required to transmit the force of a purchase to a distance object.
pitchpole	The description of a vessel that is up-ended by a heavy sea so that it turns stern over bow.
point	A division of the circumference of the magnetic compass card which is divided into 32 points; each point is 11 degrees 15 minutes.
port	The name of the left side of a vessel when a person is looking forward.
port tack	Sailing with the wind from the port side.
purchase	A mechanical device, usually consisting of two or more pulleys to increase power or force.
reach	A point of sail when the wind is from the beam. A close reach is when the wind is forward of the beam. A broad reach is when the wind is from the quarter.

reef	To reduce the area of a sail by attaching *reef points* to an adjacent spar.
reef points	Short lengths of rope attached to a sail to permit reefing the sail.
rig	A term used to describe the various arrangements of masts and sails.
rigging	All ropes, wires, or chains used to support masts and yards and to hoist, lower, and trim sails.
rudder	The most efficient means of imparting a change in direction of a vessel underway. The rudder evolved from the steering oar and presently consists of a near vertical plate that can be rotated by a tiller or wheel.
sheave	The revolving wheel in a block.
sheet	A purchase or a single line used to trim a sail.
shift	A term used to denote a change in wind direction.
shipshape	A word meaning good and seamanlike order.
shoal	A patch of water with a depth less than that of the surrounding water.
shrouds	The standing rigging of a sailing vessel that provides lateral (side-to-side) support to a mast.
snatch block	A single sheave block with a hinged side opening to permit the insertion of a rope.
spar	A general term for a wooden or metal support in the rigging of a vessel; it includes masts, yards, booms, and gaffs.
spencer	A fore-and-aft sail set on the after side of the foremast or mainmast of a square-rigged ship.
spinnaker	A three-cornered lightweight sail set forward of a yacht's headstay to increase sail area.
spreaders	Metal or wooden struts placed in pairs athwart ships on the mast to spread the angle of the upper shrouds.
sprit	A long spar extending diagonally from the base of the mast to the peak of a four-sided fore-and-aft sail.
spritsail	A (1) small square sail set under the bowsprit on early square-rigged ships and (2) four-sided fore-and-aft sail set on a sprit.
squall	A sudden gust of wind of considerable strength.
stanchion	An upright support.
standing rigging	The fixed and permanent rigging of a sailing vessel.
starboard	The right-hand side of a vessel when facing forward.
starboard tack	Sailing with the wind from the starboard side.
stay	A part of the standing rigging that supports the mast in a

fore-and-aft direction.

staysail	A triangular fore-and-aft sail that is attached to a stay.
steerageway	Sufficient forward motion to permit steering the vessel.
stem	The foremost part of the bow.
stern	The after end of the vessel.
sternway	The movement of a vessel when she is going backwards.
storm	A wind speed between forty-eight and sixty-three knots.
studding sail	An additional sail set outside square sail when the wind is light and from abaft the beam.
tack	The lower forward corner of a fore-and-aft sail.
tack	Changing direction so that the bow passes through the direction from which the wind is blowing.
tackle	Pronounced *taykle;* a purchase of two or more blocks.
taut	Tight, relating to a vessel's rigging or the hauling of ropes.
throat	The upper foremost corner of a four-sided fore-and-aft sail.
tiller	A wood or metal bar by which the rudder is rotated.
topping lift	A rope or flexible wire by which the end of a spar is hoisted or lowered.
trade wind	A steady regular wind that blows in generally a western direction in a belt between approximately 30 degrees north and 30 degrees south of the equator.
transom	The flat part of the stern in a square-sterned vessel.
underway	Even if a vessel is not making progress, a vessel is underway if its anchor is not down and holding and if the vessel is not moored to some fixed object.
wake	The disturbed column of water behind a moving vessel.
whisker pole	A short pole used to hold the clew of a jib outboard when sailing downwind on a fore-and-aft rigged vessel.
windward	The direction from which the wind is blowing.
yard	A horizontal spar attached to a mast from which a square sail is suspended.
yardarm	The outer quarter of the yard that supports a square sail.

Bibliography

Anderson, R. C., and Romola Anderson. *The Sailing Ship: Six Thousand Years of History.* London: George G. Harrap, 1947.

Angeluci, Enzo, and Attilio Cucari. *Ships.* New York: McGraw Hill, 1975.

Atkinson, Ian. *The Viking Ships.* Minneapolis: Lerner Publications, 1980.

Bathe, B. W., G. B. Rubin De Cervin, and E. Taillemite. *The Great Age of Sail.* Edited by Joseph Jobe. Translated by Michael Kelly. New York: Viking Press, 1971.

Casson, Lionel. *The Ancient Mariners.* New York: Macmillan, 1959.

———. *Illustrated History of Ships and Boats.* Garden City, N. Y.: Doubleday, 1964.

———. *Ships and Seamanship in the Ancient World.* Princeton: Princeton University Press, 1971.

Chapelle, Howard I. *The Baltimore Clipper.* New York: Edward W. Sweetman, 1968.

———. *The Search for Speed under Sail, 1700–1855.* New York: Bonanza Books, 1967.

Chatterton, E. Keble. *Sailing Ships: The Story of Their Development from the Earliest Times to the Present Day.* London: Sidwick and Jackson, 1909.

Clark, Arthur H. *The Clipper Ship Era.* Riverside, Conn.: 7 C's Press, 1910.

Conner, Dennis. *Comeback: My Race for the America's Cup.* New York: St. Martin's Press, 1987.

Conner, Dennis, and Michael Levitt. *The America's Cup.* New York: St. Martin's Press, 1998.

Dodd, Edward. *Polynesian Seafaring.* New York: Dodd Mead, 1972.

Ebsen, Buddy, with George A. Guston. *Polynesian Concept.* London: Prentice Hall International, 1972.

Harland, John. *Seamanship in the Age of Sail.* Annapolis: Naval Institute Press, 1987.

Johnstone, Paul. *The Sea Craft of Prehistory.* Cambridge: Harvard University Press, 1980.

Kemp, Peter. *The History of Ships.* London: Orbis, 1978.

Kemp, Peter, ed. *The Oxford Companion to Ships and the Sea.* London: Oxford University Press, 1976.

Kerchov, Rene. *International Marine Dictionary.* New York: Van Norstrand, 1948.

Kirsch, Peter. *The Galleon: The Great Ships of the Armada Era.* Annapolis: Naval Institute Press, 1988.

MacGregor, David R. *Schooners in Four Centuries.* Annapolis: Naval Institute Press, 1982.

Mahan, A. T. *The Influence of Sea Power upon History, 1660–1783.* New York: Dover Publications, 1987.

Maloney, Elbert S. *Chapman: Piloting, Seamanship, and Small Boat Handling.* New York: Hearst Marine Books, 1983.

Mansir, Richard A. *The Art of Ship Modeling.* New York: Van Norstrand Reinhold, 1982.

———. *A Modeler's Guide to Ancient and Medieval Ships to 1650.* Dana Point, Calif.: Moonraker Publications, 1981.

Moore, Alan. *Last Days of Mast and Sail.* Oxford: Clarendon Press, 1925.

Morison, Samuel Eliot. *The Maritime History of Massachusetts, 1783–1860.* Cambridge: The Riverside Press, 1961.

Paine, Lincoln P. *Ships of the World.* Boston: Houghton Mifflin, 1997.

Phillips-Birt, Douglas. *A History of Seamanship.* Garden City, N.Y.: Doubleday, 1971.

Ross, Wallace, with Carl Chapman. *Sail Power.* New York: Alfred A. Knopf, 1978.

Silverberg, Robert. *Nat Palmer: Antarctic Explorer and Clipper Ship Pioneer.* New York: McGraw Hill, 1967.

Stein, R. Conrad. *The Story of the Clipper Ships.* Chicago: Children's Press, 1981.

Tryckare, Tre. *The Lore of Ships.* New York: Crescent Books, 1972.

Tunis, Edwin. *Oars, Sails, and Steam.* New York: World Publishing, 1952.

Villiers, Alan. *The Battle of Trafalgar: Lord Nelson Sweeps the Sea.* New York: MacMillan,1965.

———. *Captain James Cook.* New York: Charles Scribner's and Sons, 1967.

———. *Monsoon Seas: The Story of the Indian Ocean.* New York: McGraw Hill, 1952.

Whipple, A. B. C. *The Clipper Ships.* Chicago: Time-Life Books, 1980.

Woodman, Richard. *The History of the Ship.* London: Conway Maritime Press, 1997.

Index

Note: Page numbers in *italics* indicate pages with illustrations.

About the Author

Capt. Leo Block, USNR (Ret.), a Pearl Harbor survivor, is an engineer, technical author, and sailor; history is his avocation. He left the U. S. Navy as a chief petty officer (machinist mate) and earned an engineering degree cum laude at the University of Southern California. He then served on active duty as a commissioned officer. He earned his masters in mechanical engineering also from the University of Southern California and completed the Naval War College course in strategy and policy. He has twenty U.S. patents, and his technical writings have been published in several technical magazines and in engineering society transactions. In 1992 he received an International Appliance Technical Conference Award. His articles on boating and seamanship have been published in *Sea Magazine.* His previous book, *Diesel Engines: A Boat Owners Guide to Operation and Maintenance,* now in its third printing, permitted boat owners to minimize costly engine repairs. In *To Harness the Wind,* Captain Block, who has a background in diesel and steam propulsion, discusses wind and sails as yet another propulsion system for seagoing and other vessels. Leo Block and his wife live in San Clemente, California, where he sails his thirty-foot sloop out of Dana Point and serves as an expert witness in technical litigations.